Echoes and Footprints

Echoes and Footprints

Harbert Alexander

Illustrations by Wanda Stanfill and Allison East

Copyright 2017 by Harbert Alexander

Library of Congress Cataloging-in-Publication Data

ISBN: 978-09963458-4-2

Printed and bound in the United States of America by Ingram Lightning Source.

First edition

Editor: Jacque Hillman

Editor and photographer: Jesse Hillman

Assistant editor: Katie Gould

Illustrators: Allison East and Wanda Stanfill

Cover design: Wanda Stanfill, Jacque Hillman, Jesse Hillman and Katie Gould

To contact the author, write him at
harbertalexander1@gmail.com
www.harbertalexander.com

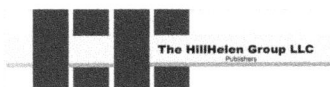

The HillHelen Group LLC
Publishers

The HillHelen Group LLC. 124 E. Baltimore St. Ste. 118
Jackson, TN 38301
www.jacquehillman.com   www.jessehillman.com

Contents

Preface and Acknowledgments

My thanks to so many people who helped bring this book to reality. Many times people ask me where I find so many stories. I am fortunate to have people around me who believe our history is all around us and call me to tell me a story or offer suggestions.

Bill King in Denmark offered help in accessing the West Tennessee Historical Papers and to give me material on Mercer and Hatchie Station.

Fred Culp, Gibson County historian, and his book *Gibson County, Past and Present* helped with the stories on Trenton, Skullbone and Fruitvale. Sadly enough, Mr. Culp passed away July 5, 2017.

Fred Birmingham introduced me to Timothy Pickering Jones. Jim Emison in Alamo sent me the material on the State of Jacksonia. Charles Blankenship lent me material on CCC Camp 499, and Myrtle Rose Emerson took us on a tour of Fruitvale and her home where she makes the "Father Christmas" figures.

Mark Harris started me on the story of Colonel Sanders and the "Twenty-Nine Chickens," and Paula Casey helped with the story of Sue Shelton White. The Frankland and Lawrence families gave the books and material on General Frankland, and as always, Evelyn Keele and Jack Woods in the Tennessee

Room of the Jackson-Madison County Library were there with help and suggestions.

Allison East and Wanda Stanfill made the stories come to life with illustrations. This book could never come to print without the help and guidance of my publisher, Jacque Hillman. Jacque and her husband, Jesse, helped edit, corrected spellings and kept us on schedule so "this book must be ready by November!"

Again my wife and partner has listened to my speeches, overlooked my piles of books and papers and given me support.

In an earlier book, I wrote about Richard Halliburton of Memphis, who asked young people to fly with him on his magic carpet. I have no magic carpet, but instead I say, "Come walk with me, and I will show you our history."

Introduction

Almost twenty years ago, I began writing monthly articles for a local newspaper. The first story was about Bill Clinton, the president. When Air Force One landed at McKellar-Sipes Regional Airport, it created a great deal of excitement and a large crowd was there to see him. Popular or not, he is still the only president to come to West Tennessee while he was in office. It was an easy story to write, but I wondered if West Tennessee had enough history to keep me writing. How wrong I was!

Echoes and Footprints is the fifth book I have written, and yet there are more stories to write and paths to follow than I could have imagined. When I first began to write about our past history, I used the expression, "Our history is all around us, if you only look." The title of this book reflects that thought when I ask readers to listen for echoes from the past. Look around you, and the footprints of those who came before us are still there.

Put on your walking shoes and come with me. First we will walk down Royal Street in Jackson, where Jefferson Davis spoke at one end of the street, and Andrew Jackson spoke at the other end near the train station. Go to Savannah near the Cherry Mansion and walk with the Cherokee Indians on the Trail of Tears. Stand with me at first light, and watch the elephants walk by one last time when Ringling Brothers came to town.

Get to know Timothy Pickering Jones, who roomed with Edgar Allan Poe at West Point, fought in two wars in Mexico and rode with Nathan Bedford Forrest in the Civil War. Talk to Colonel Harland Sanders when he lived in Jackson and worked for the railroad or walk with Sue Shelton White as she fights for passage of the Nineteenth Amendment to give women the right to vote.

As I first said twenty years ago, "Our history is all around us if you only look!" Our history is closer than you think.

Thomas Edison studies one of the light bulbs with which he lit up America. One of the world's greatest inventors, he worked as a telegraph operator at the railroad depots for some months in West Tennessee.

Chapter 1

Walking Down Royal Street

Our history is all around us, if you only look! As a historian, this has been my theme for many years. But sometimes you have to do more than look; you have to use your imagination, so close your eyes and do that with me for a few minutes. Let's take an imaginary walk down Royal Street.

Have you ever wondered how the street got that name? Do you think that Jackson once had royalty? Certainly not! In Jackson's early days, many of the prominent citizens built homes on Royal Street. However, the name "royal" was not given as a compliment. The name was first used as a sarcastic description of the fine rugs, wallpaper and furniture in some of the homes we will see as we walk down the street.

The first home we will visit is the residence of General Samuel

Facebook video library
https://goo.gl/nKdgqC

Hays at the corner of Preston and Royal. It was at this home in 1870 that Jefferson Davis, former president of the Confederacy, made his first speech after being released from Federal prison. Davis was supposed to speak at St. Luke's Episcopal Church in downtown Jackson, but the size of the crowd moved it to this site on Royal Street.

Our second stop is a business, not a home. Located from 334 to 354 North Royal, we find Southern Engine and Boiler Works, which started as a small shop to build engines and boilers. By 1900, four hundred people worked there. As a new century began, it was Jackson's largest business. In 1906, W.H. Collier, a mechanical engineer, convinced the company to begin making automobiles. Southern Engine and Boiler Works was the first company in the South to make cars from scratch. All parts of the cars were made in the plant. Between 1906 and 1910, approximately six hundred cars were made in Jackson. The cars were named Marathon and sold for about $1,500. In 1910, a group of investors bought Marathon and moved it to Nashville. Southern Engine and Boiler Works grew to be one of the largest companies of its kind until changing technology spelled its doom, and it went out of business in 1926. As we walk by the old plant site, can you hear the sounds of people working?

Going south on Royal, we begin to see Jackson's finest homes. Near the spot where Chester crosses Royal, we see the home of Dr. William E. Butler, the founder of Jackson. Known as "The Little Hermitage," the home is known for the splendor of its Oriental rugs and French wallpaper. In his later years, Dr. Butler is often seen sitting in a chair in his front yard. If it is cold, he will have a blanket on his legs. Known for his colorful language, you may hear him say, "It's too damn cold," or if it is summer, "It's too damn hot." After Dr. Butler's death in 1882, the house began to fall into disrepair. Today there is no trace of it. And yet we need to remember places like that — a home where David Crockett dined and Andrew Jackson visited, a part of our heritage.

Across the street was Dr. Butler's racetrack near where today's chamber of commerce is located. In 1843, Dr. Butler donated the land where the racetrack was located to Memphis Conference Female Institute, the forerunner of the University of Memphis Lambuth Campus.

Just down the street was the residence of Robert I. Chester, Dr. Butler's brother-in-law. Chester and Butler both married nieces of Andrew Jackson. Chester County and Chester Street are named for him.

Follow Royal, still going south, until you reach the old train station, now a museum. For a few weeks, perhaps a month, Thomas Alva Edison was a telegraph operator there. Just as the Civil War ended, he also worked in Bolivar, Grand Junction and Memphis. Though it is difficult to prove, it is intriguing to think that the greatest inventor the world has ever known once lived here. Can you hear the telegraph keys clicking?

Listen! Can you not hear the sound of marching feet going down Royal, soldiers leaving home and heading into the uncertainties of war? Listen closely; you can hear the 117th infantry regiment of the Tennessee National Guard. It is September 1940, and they will board a train for Fort Jackson,

South Carolina. They should be home in a year, but the Japanese attack on Pearl Harbor keeps them away and in uniform for five years.

At this same spot, the 6th Tennessee Infantry, boys from West Tennessee, went away to fight in the Civil War. Twelve hundred Confederate soldiers left that Sunday in May 1861. Far less than half of them would come home. Stand there by the track and think about all of the soldiers through the years who have departed from that spot.

Cross the tracks and look to the left. In front of you is Lancaster Park. It is named for Samuel C. Lancaster, one of Jackson's most famous people. An architect who conquered polio, he directed construction of the Columbia River Scenic Highway, later called Lancaster's Road in his honor.

There is a lot of magic in this area. The old well was a gathering place Sunday afternoons where parents could sit and talk while the children played nearby. Mr. Johnny's Popcorn was close by, and when the circus or the West Tennessee Fair were in town, they were here. A baseball diamond was just to the south where the Jackson Generals, our minor league team, played their home games.

Across the street and just south of the train station was Colonial Bakery. Anyone who grew up in Jackson can remember the smell of the bread as it baked. Before the bakery was built, there was a large grove of trees where politicians would speak. It was on this site in 1825 that Andrew Jackson spoke to a crowd that was estimated at larger than ten thousand people. It was his last visit to Jackson.

Jackson has a wonderful history. Take the time to travel down North Royal. Though much of it is not as it used to be, can you hear Jefferson Davis or Andrew Jackson speaking? Look to see if Dr. Butler is still sitting in his front yard. Do you see the new Marathon cars?

I hope you enjoyed our walk down Royal. More of our history resides on this street than any place I know. Close your eyes and let your imagination take hold as you begin your walk.

Between 1836 and 1839, the forced removal of the Cherokees under terrible conditions caused the deaths of nearly twenty-five percent of the tribe on the Trail of Tears.

Chapter 2

Trail of Tears

At the beginning of the 1830s, nearly 125,000 Native Americans lived on millions of acres of land in Georgia, Mississippi, Tennessee, Alabama, North Carolina and Florida. They had lived and hunted on these lands for generations. By the end of the decade, few Native Americans remained anywhere in the Southeast.

Under the banner of "Manifest Destiny," American settlers began to spread across the country with the ideology that they were destined to extend their nation across the continent. The problem was that the Native Americans were in the way!

To settlers, the Indians they encountered were unfamiliar and unfriendly. To add to the problem, the Indians occupied the ground the settlers wanted. President George Washington

Facebook video library
https://goo.gl/nKdgqC

thought the problem could be solved by civilizing and converting them to make them as much like white people as possible. The goal was to encourage them to convert to Christianity, learn to speak English and adopt the customs of the white settlers. In the Southeastern United States, many Choctaws, Chickasaws, Creeks, Seminoles and Cherokees adopted these customs and became known as the five civilized tribes. The issue was the Native Americans still occupied the land the settlers wanted.

Andrew Jackson, long an advocate of Indian removal, had spent years in campaigns against the Creeks in Georgia and Alabama and against the Seminoles in Florida. As president, he continued this crusade when he signed the Indian Removal Act of 1830, which gave the federal government the right to exchange Native American-held land in the South for land in present-day Oklahoma.

The law required the government to negotiate removal treaties fairly, voluntarily and peacefully. This was often not the way negotiations were carried out, as Native Americans were forced to vacate land they had lived on for generations.

In the winter of 1831, the Choctaws, under threat of invasion from the U.S. Army, became the first to be expelled from their land altogether. Fifteen thousand people with one thousand slaves made the move in three stages. The first group left in the fall of 1831 with little food or provisions and suffered through what was called the blizzard of 1831-1832 and the cholera epidemic of 1832. About 2,500 died on the trail, called by their leaders as the "Trail of Tears and Death." The Choctaws ceded over 11 million acres of their land in Alabama, Arkansas and Mississippi.

The Creek Indian Nation was once one of the largest and most powerful groups in the Southwest, controlling millions of acres of land in Georgia, Alabama and Florida.

In 1814, Major General Andrew Jackson led an expedition against the Creeks, climaxing at the Battle of Horseshoe Bend in Alabama near the Georgia state line. The military strength of the Creeks was virtually destroyed. As a result, the Creeks were forced to sign the Treaty of Fort Jackson in which they ceded 21 million acres of land — about one-half of the state of Alabama and twenty percent of Georgia.

Although some Creeks continued to migrate to Oklahoma in small family groups as late as the 1850s, government-sponsored removal ended in 1838. By the end of the removal, more than 23,000 Creeks migrated from the Southwest to Indian lands in Oklahoma.

The Chickasaws seemed to be the quickest of the five so-called civilized tribes to adopt European-American practices: establishing schools, converting to Christianity and building homes like the white settlers. They were peaceful and compatible with the arriving settlers. But they occupied land that the new immigrants wanted. The Chickasaws were in the way and needed to be moved.

In 1786, the Chickasaws signed the Treaty of Hopewell, which stated: "The hatchet shall be forever buried, and the peace given by the United States of America, and friendship reestablished. ..."

But President Andrew Jackson in 1830 informed the Chickasaws they only had two choices — move west or submit to the laws of the state of Mississippi. The Chickasaw chiefs, at the Treaty of Pontotoc Creek, ceded the remainder of their land to the United States and agreed to move to Oklahoma. Unlike other tribes, the Chickasaws were paid cash for their land, rather than receiving land in Oklahoma. On July 4, 1837, three thousand Chickasaws with all of their slaves, wagons and livestock gathered in Memphis to begin the move west. Sadly enough, more than five hundred died of smallpox and dysentery during the trip.

After the United States acquired Florida from Spain in 1819, settlers began the move to acquire the land owned and occupied by the Seminole Indians. At first, the tribe was moved into a large reservation of the Florida Peninsula in the Treaty of Moultrie Creek in 1823. Nine years later, at the Treaty of Payne's Landing, the Seminoles were evicted and forced to move to Indian lands in Oklahoma.

The Cherokee removal from their lands in Georgia, North Carolina, South Carolina, Tennessee, Texas and Alabama took place from 1836 to 1839. Being forced to move west to Oklahoma, the Cherokees faced extreme weather with little food or clothing, which caused the deaths of an estimated four thousand Cherokees. This portion of Native American forced evacuation is often called "The Trail of Tears."

Of the sixteen thousand Cherokees, about twenty-five percent of the tribe were lost. During the journey the people would sing "Amazing Grace" to improve morale. The song has become an anthem of the Cherokee people.

Some Cherokees who lived on private land, rather than tribal land, were allowed to remain. Approximately fifteen hundred remained on private land in the Great Smoky Mountains.

The Trail of Tears is often considered to be one of the most regrettable episodes in American history. The Trail of Tears National Historic Trail was designated by the U.S. Congress in 1987. It stretches across nine states for 2,200 miles.

When the first settlers came into West Tennessee in the 1820s, it was considered to be "the land of the Chickasaws." Archaeological surveys have identified hundreds of Native American village sites, a majority of which are located near or adjacent to the Tennessee, Obion, Forked Deer and Wolf rivers and their tributaries. Many of these sites date back five to six thousand years or more.

There is, however, little evidence of Chickasaw villages. Early travelers, such as the Williams family, who came through North Mississippi into West Tennessee in the 1820s, describe traveling through the Choctaw Nation and then the Chickasaw before reaching West Tennessee. Because there were few Native Americans in West Tennessee when the earliest settlers arrived, there was no necessity for their removal.

West Tennessee is part of the Trail of Tears, however. Six hundred Cherokees with fifty-six wagons and 318 horses, known as Bell's Treaty Party, headed south on October 11, 1838, from the Cherokee Agency along the Hiwassee River. The party was accompanied by a military escort under the command of U.S. Army Lieutenant Edward Deas and Cherokee Chief John Bell. It was the only Cherokee detachment to be accompanied by the military. They traveled to Chattanooga where they crossed the

Tennessee River at Ross's Landing. After crossing the Tennessee River twice more, they climbed the Cumberland Plateau at Monteagle. Three more times they crossed the Tennessee River before reaching Savannah, where they crossed the river once again at the ferry landing near the Cherry Mansion.

The group then followed the Old State Road to Purdy to Bethel Springs to Memphis. Their 89-day journey ended on January 7, 1839, when they reached the Cherokee Nation's border west of Evansville, Arkansas.

In 2004 Senator Sam Brownback, a Republican from Kansas, introduced Senate Joint Resolution 37 "to offer an apology to all Native Peoples on behalf of the United States for past ill-conceived policies by the United States Government regarding Indian Tribes." It passed in February 2008.

Perhaps it had to happen. For the country to grow and become what it is today, it probably had to happen. For the Native Americans to have dual occupancy of the land with the new immigrants would probably not have worked. Still, it is a sad story. America has done many great things. The forced removal of the Indians was not one of them.

Andrew Jackson visited Jackson at least two times during various bids for the presidency. In 1824, he had the highest number of Electoral College votes and the largest number of popular votes, but he was still not elected president.

Chapter 3

Election Surprise

In September 1825, Andrew Jackson came to visit the little river town that was named for him. It was his first visit to Jackson despite the fact that his wife's sister, Jane Donelson Hays, lived here. It was a celebration for three days with speeches and dinners. And yet behind his smile and confident air, something was amiss.

In the presidential election of 1824, less than a year previously, Andrew Jackson had been elected president of the United States. Or had he? Jackson received 99 Electoral College votes. John Quincy Adams had 84, William H. Crawford had 41 and Henry Clay had 37. Jackson had the largest number of popular votes as well with more than 150,000 votes. Adams had 108,000 and Crawford and Clay each had less than 50,000. Clearly Andrew

Facebook video library
https://goo.gl/nKdgqC

Jackson had been elected as president. He had the highest number of Electoral College votes. He had the largest number of popular votes. But he had not been elected as president!

In 1824, the law specified that the candidate must win a majority of the votes, not the highest number. Accordingly, the matter then went to the House of Representatives to be decided.

According to the Twelfth Amendment, only the top three candidates were admitted. Clay was deleted. As Clay despised Jackson, he threw his support to Adams, who won the election. Thirteen states voted for Adams, seven for Jackson and four for Crawford. Thus, Jackson became the only presidential candidate to receive the most Electoral College votes, win the popular election and not be elected. Despite this setback, he turned his attention to the future and was elected president in 1828 and 1832.

Four other candidates would be elected as president despite not winning the popular vote. To win the election, the candidates must have the most Electoral College votes regardless of how they did on the popular vote.

When Americans vote for a president and vice president, they are actually voting for presidential electors, known collectively as the Electoral College. It is these electors, chosen by the people, who elect the chief executive. The Constitution assigns each state a number of electors equal to the combined total of the state's Senate and House of Representatives delegations. Currently there are 538 electors.

Four elections would follow where one of the candidates received the largest number of popular votes but lost the election.

In 1876 Rutherford Hayes had 250,000 fewer popular votes

than Samuel Tilden. Hayes had the most Electoral College votes with the narrowest of margins, 185-184. As a result, Hayes won the presidency by one vote!

Twelve years later, Benjamin Harrison defeated Grover Cleveland despite having 90,000 fewer popular votes. Harrison had 233 Electoral College votes compared to 168 for Cleveland.

In 2000, George W. Bush defeated Albert Gore Jr. with 271 electoral votes. Gore trailed with five less at 266. It is intriguing that had Gore won the electoral votes in Tennessee, his home state, he would have been elected president! Gore received more than 500,000 popular votes than Bush.

One last presidential hopeful suffered a similar fate when Hillary Clinton was ahead of Donald Trump in 2016 by nearly three million popular votes, thanks in large part to California, but lost the election when Trump had 304 votes in the Electoral College to Clinton's 227.

Though Andrew Jackson was furious when he came to Jackson in 1825, he moved on, getting ready for his next chance to be president. Ten years later, another politician came to Jackson. His name was David Crockett, and he had just been defeated by Adam Huntsman in the race for the congressional seat formerly held by Crockett. Losing the election ruined his chances for running for president. It also cost him his life! When asked what he would do next, he responded, "You can go to hell for I am going to Texas!" Six months later, Crockett was dead at The Alamo.

Much of our history revolves around politics. Winners and losers alike, they create the stories for future generations. Who do you think our next president will be?

Sue Shelton White of Jackson, the only Tennessee suffragist to be thrown into jail, campaigned relentlessly for the passage of the Nineteenth Amendment when Tennessee voted to ratify, thus giving women across America the right to vote.

Chapter 4

Sue Shelton White, Tennessee Suffragist, and the Nineteenth Amendment's Passage

History often repeats itself. Though time has passed, and the characters are not the same, the patterns are similar and often lead to results that duplicate those of another time.

On January 21, 2017, the day after Donald Trump was sworn in as the forty-fifth president of the United States, more than 200,000 women marched and demonstrated in Washington, D.C. Some estimates were as high as 500,000! More than 6,000 marched in Memphis with similar results in other major cities.

Jubilant and excited in the sunshine of an unseasonably warm January day, the women wanted a display intended to show the new president and the Republican Congress that they were united on issues important to them.

Facebook video library
https://goo.gl/nKdgqC

In 1919, nearly a century ago, a young woman joined a march with other members of the National Woman's Party in Washington to show support for passage of the Nineteenth Amendment, the right of women to vote. The woman's name was Sue Shelton White.

She was born in Henderson, Tennessee, on May 25, 1887, the second of three children. Her father was a Methodist minister and lawyer. When she was nine years old, her father died. Four years later, when her mother died, she was taken in by an aunt.

Three years later, White took a teacher training course at Georgia Robertson Christian College (now Freed-Hardeman University) and attended West Tennessee Business College the following year.

At the end of the school year, she began her career as a stenographer and clerk for the Southern Engine and Boiler Works. At the time, it was one of the largest businesses in Jackson with more than four hundred employees. After she had been employed there for a year, the company began to manufacture Marathon automobiles, becoming the first company in the South to do so. Despite the company's success, White was offered little chance for promotion. In 1907, she left the Southern Engine and Boiler Works and succeeded her sister as Jackson's court reporter.

Stymied by her inability to achieve her dream of earning a law degree, White became active in the Tennessee Equal Suffrage Association. Over the next five years, she became convinced that the policies and methods of the more radical National Woman's Party were more effective and changed her allegiance, moving to Washington, where she became editor for the NWP's national paper, called *The Suffragist*.

On February 19, 1919, White drew national attention while participating in one of the NWP's "Silent Sentinels" demonstrations in front of the White House when she burned a paper effigy of President Woodrow Wilson.

As the paper effigy of President Wilson turned to ashes, the police stepped in and arrested thirty-nine demonstrators. After a night in jail, White and twenty-seven others were sentenced to five days in jail. Following their release, they boarded a train, the "Prison Special," which carried them wearing mock prison uniforms through the country for twenty-six days.

After Congress passed the Nineteenth Amendment on June 4, 1919, White returned to Tennessee and participated in the fight for state ratification. By Saturday, August 7, 1920, The Hermitage Hotel in Nashville had become a whirling center of the debate with crowds of pro- and anti-suffrage forces gathered to lobby and count votes.

On August 9, 1920, the Tennessee Legislature met in special session to vote on the Nineteenth Amendment, which would grant women the right to vote. Thirty-five states had already approved it. Twelve states had voted against it. A three-fourths vote of the forty-eight states was required for it to pass. Tennessee was the last to vote and it could only pass if Tennessee voted for it.

The Woman's Suffrage Movement had been going on for seventy-two years, and yet it appeared that passage of the amendment was doubtful at best.

On the morning of the vote, the capitol was full and the crowd overflowed out onto the street. Women wore white dresses with yellow sashes. Men who were opposed to passage wore red roses.

For those who kept score, it appeared the amendment would fall short by one vote. But then an element of surprise crept into the proceedings! Representative Harry Burn, wearing a red rose, had received a letter that morning from his mother in Niota, Tennessee, asking him to vote for the amendment. Torn with indecision, Representative Burn took his seat.

In a move designed to ensure the bill did not pass, Speaker Seth Walker moved for the amendment to be tabled. If it was tabled, the debate would be over, and the amendment defeated.

But then, the unexpected began to happen. To use an old magician's expression, the rabbit jumped out of the hat! At first the roll-call vote went as expected. Harry Burn, despite his mother's urging, voted for tabling. The vote stood at 48-47 in favor of tabling when Banks Turner of Yorkville in Gibson County stood up. He had not responded when his name was called previously. In a loud voice, he said, "I wish to be recorded as against the motion to table." The vote was 48-48, and the motion to table was defeated. The Nineteenth Amendment was still alive!

Speaker Walker called for a recount. Moving onto the floor, Walker sat down and put his arm around Banks Turner, continuing to tell him to vote for tabling. When Turner's name was called, he again voted against the tabling and the vote stood at 48-48.

Now the vote on the original motion to pass the Nineteenth Amendment began. Even with Banks Turner voting for the amendment, it was obvious it would not pass without one more vote to give it a majority of 49.

This time Harry Burn took his mother's advice and voted "aye." Thanks to Burn, Banks Turner and the stalwart efforts of Joe Hanover, the floor leader who kept the pro-suffrage votes together, the vote passed. A sea of yellow rose petals cascaded down from the galleries above the floor as the suffragists celebrated. After decades of struggle, women had won the right to vote.

Shortly after ratification, Senator Kenneth D. McKellar appointed White as his clerk and secretary. While working for Senator McKellar, White attended Washington College of Law, earning her law degree in 1923.

In 1926, she moved back to Jackson to join with Hu Anderson in the law firm of Anderson and White. She was the first female attorney in Madison County.

In 1932, White returned to Washington when President Franklin Roosevelt appointed her as executive assistant to Molly Rumsey in the Consumer Division of the National Recovery Administration. In 1935, she moved to the newly organized Social Security Administration and served as attorney to help implement the Social Security Act.

After a long bout with cancer, Sue Shelton White died in May 1943. She had come a long way from West Tennessee to Washington. It had been a hard fight for women's rights, and she had played a big part in it.

And once again, women march in Washington and across the country to protect and to preserve the dignity and equality of women. Sue Shelton White has been dead for nearly seventy-five years, but her legacy lives on wherever women march.

Thomas Pickering Jones, graduate of the
United States Military Academy at West
Point, was a roommate of Edgar Allan Poe.
Jones fought in multiple wars with General
Sam Houston, David Crockett and Nathan
Bedford Forrest but lived to the ripe old
age of 90 in Texas.

Chapter 5

Soldier of Texas, Soldier of the South

To read about the life of Timothy Pickering Jones is like reading fiction. Can you imagine the life of one man that included Edgar Allan Poe, David Crockett, Sam Houston and Nathan Bedford Forrest?

He was born in North Carolina but moved to Jackson, Tennessee, when he was a boy. The family settled in a large tract of land east of Jackson on Jones Creek adjacent to the home of Adam Huntsman.

In 1830 Jones entered the United States Military Academy at West Point. One of his two roommates was Edgar Allan Poe. Prior to entering West Point, Poe had spent a semester at the University of Virginia after which he served a short period in the army. Both Poe and Jones entered West Point on July 1, 1830.

Facebook video library
https://goo.gl/nKdgqC

Jones would later say, "I realized even in my young years that he was an exceptionally brilliant fellow, studying but little, but always perfect in recitations, save in mathematics which he boldly declared had no place in the brain of an intellectual man —too dull and commonplace. The strict discipline, the mathematical requirements of the military school, kept my friend in an unhappy frame of mind." Poe struggled with life at West Point and was dismissed March 6, 1831, vowing he would spend the remainder of his life as a writer.

Jones graduated from West Point in 1835. When he returned to West Tennessee, he got caught up in the excitement of the westward movement and made plans to accompany David Crockett to Texas. When Crockett's departure was delayed, Jones joined another company and headed west, crossing the Sabine River on his twenty-first birthday. Upon reaching Nacogdoches, he joined a company called "The Boys From the Red Lands" or "The Red Land Force." Jones was elected lieutenant, and the company headed west in hopes of reinforcing troops at Coleta and Goliad. While they were en route, General Sam Houston intercepted them and tried to stop them, saying he had ordered The Alamo to be destroyed and abandoned and for the Americans at Goliad to retreat. Many of the Tennessee soldiers did as requested and turned back east. Some of the "Red Land Force" went ahead to Goliad where they were captured and executed.

By being ahead of Crockett, Jones had missed certain death at The Alamo. Through the intervention of Houston, he had missed death once again. When the war was over, Jones returned home to West Tennessee where he remained until 1846 when war with

Mexico erupted. Returning to Texas, he was elected as a captain of Company F of the 2nd Tennessee Volunteers. Marching into Mexico with General Zachary Taylor, he crossed the Rio Grande at Matamoros and was involved in all of the fighting between there and Tampico. After the American victory, Jones again returned to West Tennessee and resumed the life of a planter.

When the Civil War broke out, he again put on a uniform and prepared to go to war. Elected lieutenant colonel of the 6th Tennessee, he was in command of Company H of the Southern Guards, men from Madison County. Their "baptism of fire" came on the first day of the Battle of Shiloh, when the regiment was ordered to advance against an area known as "The Hornets' Nest." Concealed in the woods was the 14th Iowa Regiment. When Jones' men were within thirty paces of the woods, the Iowa soldiers opened fire. Jones' horse was killed, but he was not seriously injured. By his account, 194 Confederates were killed instantly. Other accounts were as high as 250 killed. When the Battle of Shiloh was over, the 6th Tennessee had lost more than 500 men killed or wounded!

After the 6th and 9th Tennessee regiments were combined due to heavy losses, Jones served under Forrest until the war ended.

After the war, Tim returned to Jackson and lived here until 1882 when he moved to Texas. It was his third time to go there. Once he followed Crockett. Once again, he went there as a soldier. This time he followed family and lived with a daughter until he died at the age of ninety. His obituary in a Texas newspaper concluded with "Peace to Thy Ashes, Old Warrior."

Ernest Frankland, who became a legend at the Battle of Mortain during World War II, distinguished himself in military service by rising to the rank of general. His list of medals begins with the Distinguished Service Cross.

Chapter 6

Ernest Frankland, the Fighting Colonel

The 30th Infantry Division is named the "Old Hickory" Division after Andrew Jackson. Its history goes back to 1774 when East Tennessee militia men helped to defeat Indians at the Battle of Point Pleasant. Since then, the division has participated in every war in which the United States has been involved including the Revolutionary War, the War of 1812, the Civil War, Spanish-American War and the war with Mexico.

The First Battalion of the 117th Infantry, 30th Division, came into existence in 1917. During the First World War, they were heavily involved, especially when they broke through the Hindenburg Line, a victory that hastened the end of the war. Twelve men of the 30th received Congressional Medals of Honor. When the war was over, the 30th was deactivated from

Federal service and reverted to its National Guard role.

As war clouds gathered in 1940, Americans relied on President Roosevelt's promise that no American soldier would fight again in Europe. December 7, 1941, and Pearl Harbor changed that! But when the 30th Division was called into active duty on September 16, 1940, fifteen months before Pearl Harbor, fighting the German army was of little concern.

Going off to war was an old tradition in West Tennessee. Men had been marching down Royal Street and boarding trains at the N.C. & St. L. Railroad Depot since the Civil War when the 6th Tennessee Regiment rode away to find its destiny at Shiloh.

On the morning of the 16th, members of the First Battalion assembled at the National Guard Armory. After the unit was formed, the familiar chant of "left face" and "forward march" sent them marching down Royal Street where friends and family waited for a last "goodbye." Boarding trains, the unit began the trip to Fort Jackson, South Carolina, where they remained for six months.

Over the next two years, the battalion moved from training assignments and field maneuvers at Fort Bragg, North Carolina, and Fort Benning, Georgia, to Camp Blanding, Florida. In September 1943, during maneuvers at Camp Forrest, Tennessee, Major Robert Ernest Frankland was assigned as battalion commander. Following the end of maneuvers, he was promoted to lieutenant colonel.

Colonel Frankland, known as Ernest to his friends and family, was one of five brothers from Jackson, Tennessee. His father was born in Ontario, Canada, before immigrating to Chicago and then to Jackson where he began Frankland Carriage Company. The company built horse-drawn carriages. With the coming of automobiles, the business changed to building truck bodies and cabs and also specialized in auto repair. Radio advertisements promoted the company could "fix anything on a car except its engine."

Three of the five brothers worked in the family business. Colonel Frankland's brother Walter was also a lieutenant colonel in the 117th Infantry in the Quartermaster Company. Wartime photographs show the two colonels laughing and shaking hands.

To promote secrecy, every unit in combat is given a code name. The name assigned to First Battalion, 117th Infantry, was "Curlew."

On February 12, 1944, the battalion boarded the ship John Ericsson and sailed for England. Twelve days later, they landed at Liverpool, England. Following D-Day, June 6, 1944, the unit began preparations for crossing the English Channel, which was accomplished on the night of June 13.

During the next five weeks, Curlew only spent five days attacking but was in constant contact with German defenders. Here their first casualties occurred with a significant number of dead and wounded. For months and months, the soldiers had been practicing, playing at war. But now the bullets and artillery rounds were real. And sadly enough, dead and wounded members of the First Battalion were real, too.

On July 25, after six weeks of probing the German lines, General Omar Bradley mounted "Operation Cobra," which broke through, causing the entire western half of the German front in Normandy to collapse. On August 3, as American troops continued to widen the corridor, soldiers of the Seventh Corps captured the village of Mortain.

Although Colonel Frankland had been at the front of his troops, leading and taking care of them, it was at Mortain that he became a legend. One of his soldiers described it best: "The 1st Battalion of the 117th Infantry belonged to Ernest Frankland. The small handsome National Guard officer was to lead his battalion every step of the way."

Sergeant James Waldrup from Jackson said, "He was the finest soldier I ever served with."

Operation Luttich was the code name for a German counter-attack that took place around the American positions near Mortain. The attack was made under the orders of Adolf Hitler. The Battle of Mortain lasted six days, from August 7 through August 13.

On Sunday, August 6, the battalion arrived and set up positions at Saint-Barthelemy and Mortain. Expecting little resistance, they were in for a surprise when German attacks started, just after midnight on August 7. By morning, the 117th was in danger of being destroyed. As German tanks overran their positions, two events occurred involving Colonel Frankland.

Colonel Frankland had a German tank pull up in front of an abandoned house where he had his command center. Looking out the window, Frankland saw two of his radiomen being marched out with their hands up. Armed with his .45 caliber revolver, Frankland shot and killed the two Germans guarding them. As Colonel Frankland turned to escape, the German tank commander was standing in the turret of his tank with his back to the Americans. Frankland shot the tank commander and then climbed up on the tank and killed the entire crew. Frankland never reported this incident, but two of his soldiers said, "If it had been written up, he'd have gotten the Congressional Medal of Honor. But the Colonel never reported it, no way, no shape, no form, no fashion."

Despite heavy losses, Frankland's battalion would survive. It had inflicted far heavier losses on the attacking Panzer divisions. More importantly, it had delayed the main thrust of the German attack for six hours. A book about the 30th Division said, "Surprised, outnumbered, and largely unsupported, the defenders of St. Barthelemy turned the tide of the Battle of Mortain in a forgotten struggle that ranks as one of the epic engagements of World War II."

And yet the price was high. On the morning of the 7th, actual casualties totaled 263 men, nearly two-thirds of the battalion's fighting strength.

The war would continue and, with it, more casualties. The Battle of the Bulge lay just ahead in the winter of 1944-1945. When the war finally ended in 1945, the 117th Infantry boarded troop ships and headed home to the United States and Tennessee.

For his action at Saint Barthelemy Colonel Frankland received the Distinguished Service Cross. This was just the beginning! The Silver Star Medal followed; a Bronze Star was next, followed by a Bronze Star with Oak Leaf Clusters and then another Bronze Star with additional Oak Leaf Clusters. This final medal was a Croix De Guerre medal in January 1945.

When Colonel Frankland returned home, he went to work in the family business. He was active in the Jackson community and Frankland Carriage Company, and few people knew of his service in World War II.

Colonel Frankland continued his military service in the Tennessee National Guard. When he finally retired, he had served for thirty-four years and had risen to the rank of major general!

Today, General Frankland's pistol is locked up in a safe along with his service records and military honors. Can you imagine holding that pistol? Pretend you were there that morning, August 7, 1944, when German tanks came crashing in through the fog.

Pretend you had to use it to kill two German soldiers and an entire tank crew. With that pistol and with his leadership, he saved the men of his battalion from the German onslaught. America has many heroes. General Ernest Frankland was one of them.

On June 4, 2000, the National Guard Armory was dedicated to Major General Robert Ernest Frankland and Brigadier General Abner Utley Taylor.

Author and soldier Leander Stillwell began
his military career as a teenager. On January
6, 1862, Stillwell enlisted as a private in
Company D of the 61st Illinois Infantry.

Chapter 7

Leander Stillwell, a Yankee Soldier in West Tennessee

In 1916, more than half a century after the end of the Civil War, Leander Stillwell began to write his story of life as a soldier in the Union Army. In 1920 he published "The Story of a Common Soldier of Army Life in the Civil War, 1861-1865."

When the Civil War began, Leander Stillwell was eighteen years old. One of twelve children, he lived with his parents in a log cabin on a small farm near Otter Creek, Illinois, in La Salle County between the Illinois and Mississippi rivers.

On July 21, 1861, Union forces suffered a crushing defeat in Virginia in the Battle of Bull Run. Following this, President Abraham Lincoln issued a call for five hundred thousand

Facebook video library
https://goo.gl/nKdgqC

volunteers, and Northern states began organizing regiments.

As the summer drew to a close, Leander told his father, "It was the duty of every young fellow to go for a soldier and help save the nation. It was simply intolerable to stay at home, among the girls and be pointed at by soldiers as a stay-at-home coward."

Leander's father, though frightened that his son would be killed or crippled, gave him permission to "join up." His only request was for Leander to help sow the winter wheat, gather the corn and lay in a large supply of wood for the winter.

On Monday morning, January 6, 1862, Leander rode a mule twenty miles north to Camp Carrollton, Illinois, where he enlisted as a private in Company D of the 61st Illinois Infantry. After a brief physical, he put on his new uniform for the first time. It would be four years before he took it off. Given a two-day furlough, he returned home. When his father saw him in the new uniform, he simply said, "Well, I reckon you've done right."

When the news arrived of the Confederate defeat and surrender at Fort Donelson, it was met with mixed feelings: Pride and excitement at first, but then fear this would end the war, and they would be discharged and sent home like "trundle bed soldiers and have to sit around and hear sure enough warriors tell the stories of actual war and fighting."

Little did they know!

After weeks of marching and drilling, the regiment received orders to leave Camp Carrollton and proceed to Alton, Illinois, to load onto steamboats that carried them fifteen miles on the

Mississippi River to Benton Barracks in St. Louis, where they remained for the next four weeks.

On March 25, the 61st Illinois with nine hundred men departed from St. Louis and headed for the front. Up to this time, Leander Stillwell had never been more than twenty-five miles from home. Two days later they were at Cairo, Illinois, and from there they traveled up the Ohio River to the mouth of the Tennessee River on the evening of March 31, when they became a part of the Army of Tennessee under the command of General U.S. Grant.

Upon arrival, the regiment marched about two miles away from the landing and went into camp between the 18th Missouri and the 18th Wisconsin. Six days later when the Battle of Shiloh began, the camp of the 61st was one of the first to be overrun by Confederate soldiers. Fighting and falling back as best they could, by the end of the day they were close to the road coming up from Pittsburg Landing.

It had been a long, hard day for the young soldiers, their first time to come under fire, and their first time to witness the death of a friend in combat. The unit was held in reserve the second day. When they returned to the wreckage of their camp, eighty of their comrades were not with them, having been killed or wounded.

Following the Battle of Shiloh, the 61st took part in the siege of Corinth, Mississippi. After the Confederate withdrawal south to Tupelo, Union soldiers began the occupation of West Tennessee.

In early June, the 61st Illinois left their camp on Owl Creek near Corinth and turned north toward Jackson. At first they stopped in Bethel Springs for several weeks. A few days after they were in camp, Leander received a letter from home that every soldier dreads: A newspaper clipping that his sweetheart had married another!

Departing Bethel Springs on June 16, the regiment marched to Jackson where they remained for a month. Federal soldiers first occupied Jackson on June 7 when the 78th Ohio and the 30th Illinois arrived, taking control of the two railroad depots and the telegraph office. Union forces, sometimes numbering in the thousands, would remain in Jackson for a year.

Following their stay in Jackson, the 61st turned south and marched to Bolivar where they set up camp. Their primary duty was to guard the railroad from the bridge over the Hatchie River north to the station at Toone, a distance of about seven miles.

On the afternoon of December 15, the regiment was loaded onto boxcars and taken to Jackson, arriving a little before sundown. As the weather was unusually warm, overcoats and blankets were left behind. After marching about two miles east of Jackson, they stopped in an old field near a small country graveyard named Salem Cemetery where they bivouacked for the night.

Shortly after dark, the weather turned bitter cold. As they were without coats and blankets, they suffered through the night. In Leander's own words:

"Along in the evening the weather turned intensely cold. It was a clear, starlit night, and the stars glittered in the heavens

like little icicles. We were strictly forbidden to build any fires, for the reason, as our officers truly said, the Confederates were not more than a half mile away, right in our front. As before stated, we had no blankets, and how we suffered with the cold! I shall never forget that night of December 18th, 1862. We would form little columns of twenty or thirty men, in two ranks, and would just trot around and round in the tall weeds and broom sedge to keep from chilling to death. Sometimes we would pile down on the ground in great bunches, and curl up close together like hogs, in our efforts to keep warm. But some part of our bodies would be exposed, which soon would be stinging with cold, then up we would get and renew the trotting process. ... But the hours seemed interminably long, and it looked like the night would never come to an end. At last some little woods birds were heard, faintly chirping in the weeds and underbrush nearby, then some owls set up a hooting in the woods behind us, and I knew that dawn was approaching."

Nathan Bedford Forrest led the Confederate forces north of the cemetery as he began his 1862 raid into West Tennessee. On the day before near Lexington, Forrest had soundly defeated two Union regiments, capturing two Union artillery pieces. Forrest's plan was to bluff an attack on Jackson, forcing the Union army to concentrate their forces there, while he turned north into Gibson County.

With the coming of the dawn, the 61st Illinois moved to a slight rise at the back of the cemetery behind a split rail fence. On the other side of the road, the 43rd Illinois was hidden in a large group of trees.

What happened next is best described by Leander Stillwell:

"Suddenly, without a note of warning, and not preceded by even a skirmish line, there appeared coming over the ridge in front and down the road, a long column of Confederate cavalry! They were, when first seen, at a walk, and marching by the flank with a front of four men. How deep the column was we could not tell. The word was immediately passed down our line not to fire until at the word of command, and that we were to fire by file, beginning on the right. That is only, two men, front and rear rank, would fire together, and so on, down the line. The object of this was apparent: by the time the left of the regiment had emptied their guns, the right would have reloaded, and thus a continuous firing would be maintained. With guns cocked and fingers on the triggers, we waited in tense anxiety for the word to fire. ... Finally, when they were in fair musket range, came the order, cool and deliberate, without a trace of excitement: "At-ten-shun, bat-tal-yun! Fire by file! Ready! — Commence firing!" and down the line crackled the musketry. Concurrently with us, the old 43rd Illinois on the right joined in the serenade. In the front file of the Confederate column was one of the usual fellows with more daring than discretion who was mounted on a tall, white horse. Of course, as long as that horse was on its feet, everybody shot at him, or the rider. But that luckless steed soon went down in a cloud of dust, and that was the end of old Whitey. The effect of our fire on the enemy was marked and instantaneous. The head of their column crumpled up instanter, the road was full of dead

and wounded horses, while several that were riderless went galloping down the road by us, with bridle reins and stirrups flapping on their necks and flanks. I think there is no doubt that the Confederates were taken completely by surprise. They shopped short when we opened on them, wheeled around, and went back much faster than they came, except a little bunch who had been dismounted. They hoisted a white rag, came in, and surrendered. The whole affair was exceedingly "short and sweet ..."

After the fight at Salem Cemetery, the 61st remained in Jackson until late January, when they returned to their old camp in Bolivar. In the middle of May, they turned south to be a part of the siege of Vicksburg. They had been in West Tennessee for eleven months. The last Union soldiers left West Tennessee on June 7, 1865.

Leander Stillwell continued his service with the 61st Illinois until the end of the war. He was never wounded or seriously injured. By 1865 he had risen from the rank of private to first lieutenant.

Returning home, he resumed his work on the family farm before going back to school and earning a law degree. He practiced law in Illinois and Kansas before being elected as a judge in Illinois. He married, had five children and lived to the age of ninety-one.

If you go to Old Salem Cemetery on Cotton Grove Road, stand at the back of the cemetery and look east down the road where Forrest's cavalry appeared. It is the same as it was in 1862, and Leander's description will bring it back to life. Close your eyes and use your imagination. Perhaps you will hear the sound of Forrest's cavalry as they come down the road. Look for the soldier on the white horse at the head of the column. And where you are standing, imagine the sound of Union rifles as Leander and the 61st Illinois begin to fire their rifles.

In 1920, an aging Leander Stillwell published "The Story of a Common Soldier of Army Life in the Civil War, 1861-1865."

Elephants were once premium entertainers when the Ringling Bros. and Barnum & Bailey, "The Greatest Show on Earth," came to town.

Chapter 8

Farewell to the Elephants

They came at first light. Huge and magnificent, especially for a small boy with a tight grip on his father's hand. They were elephants, the largest land mammal in the world. They were circus elephants, some weighing more than eight thousand pounds.

The circus had come to town, Ringling Bros. and Barnum & Bailey, "The Greatest Show on Earth" was back! They had come in at night, by trains, and now they were unloading. The elephants came first as they moved to the nearby circus grounds. I could hear the roar of the big cats, the lions and tigers still on the train in their special cars. Despite the assurance of a parent's hand, I always wondered what would happen if one got loose. And I hoped it wouldn't happen today!

Facebook video library
https://goo.gl/nKdgqC

What do you remember about Ringling Brothers? You need to be at least sixty years old to remember when the circus traveled by train. July 1956 was the end of the traveling across the countryside and putting up the big canvas tents. This, of course, ended the parade from the train to the circus grounds. No longer would the circus move from town to town but showed only in larger towns with fixed facilities. No more canvas tents, but large municipal facilities.

Circuses still travel across West Tennessee but not quite like what they used to be. They are much smaller and are used primarily to promote some type of charity. Several weeks ago, I took my six-year-old granddaughter to a circus. It was a little smaller than I remembered. Actually, it was much smaller — three jugglers and a monkey made up the cast. The crowd was smaller, less than a hundred people. Still, they had cotton candy and popcorn, and the children laughed and loved it.

As we watched that little circus, my thoughts traveled back to when Ringling Brothers was in West Tennessee and the parts I liked best. Not one ring, not two rings but three rings "under the big top." Vendors everywhere with candy apples, cotton candy and big helium balloons. Men and women high above swinging on trapezes while others walked on tight ropes below.

The lions and tigers were the main attraction with Jack "Bring Them Back Alive" Buck making them perform. Elephants seemed to be everywhere, and in the far ring a tiny car drove up. When they opened the door, fifteen or so clowns got out. How did they all get in there? It puzzles me still. And walking slowly at the edge of the crowd was a sad clown, so sad he would make you want to hug him, to tell him things would get better. His name was Emmett Kelly, or "Woeful Willie" — the most famous clown of all time.

Despite its popularity, Ringling Brothers had suffered a number of setbacks. On July 6, 1944, in Hartford, Connecticut, in an afternoon performance, the large canvas tent caught on fire, and 167 people lost their lives in one of the worst fire disasters in American history. As a result, Ringling Brothers management set aside all of its profits for the next ten years to pay claims filed against the show by survivors and the city of Hartford.

More problems followed. The circus has a veterinary staff to take care of the animals. In 1995 the circus opened the Center for Elephant Conservation in Florida. More than fifty elephants are housed there.

Many animal welfare and animal rights groups oppose the use of wild animals in circuses. For more than a decade, Ringling Brothers was involved in a lawsuit alleging mistreatment of the elephants used in the performances. Despite the fact that the suit was dismissed, circus management elected to stop using elephants in its shows. The final show with elephants occurred on May 1, 2016.

On January 14, 2017, it was announced that the circus would be closed in May. Rising costs and declining attendance, after the elephants were retired, were given as reasons for closing. The last shows were rescheduled for May 21, 2017.

Ringling Brothers, "The Greatest Show on Earth," has been

a part of our culture for nearly a hundred and fifty years. Not so for future generations of children who will never see the performing elephants, lions and tigers or even a sad-faced clown named "Woeful Willie." But for those of us who were once children, it was a magical day when the circus came to town.

Clown Emmett Kelly was a famous figure during the heyday of the traveling circus.

Many years after World War II at a business event, a Japanese soldier
(above) met Pat Hitchcock, who had been a P.O.W. in a Japanese
prison camp. They did not speak.

Chapter 9

My Friend Pat

As a West Tennessee historian and storyteller, I continue to be amazed at the diversity of people who pass through West Tennessee. It has always been that way since the early pioneer days and continues so today.

One day, about thirty years ago, I met Pat Hitchcock. He had come to Jackson with one of the large industrial companies. He had a big contagious smile and upon meeting him, you would guess he had always lived here.

As I got to know him better, I found an unexpected chapter of his life, one he didn't talk about at first. Instead, he preferred to talk about the land he had purchased in Middle Tennessee. As a promotion, Jack Daniel would sell a few inches of land to friends of the distillery and send glowing reports each year of

Facebook video library
https://goo.gl/nKdgqC

how their investment was doing.

It was some time later when Pat told me he was writing a book. The book came out in 1996 with the title *Forty Months in Hell*. Pat Hitchcock was a Japanese prisoner of war for almost three and a half years!

Pat grew up in Minneapolis. In June of his freshman year, he "graduated" from St. Thomas College. As he put it, "I felt there was nothing they could teach me about the real world and they agreed."

He moved to California, where he went to work in a factory. Again, in Pat's words, "I learned how deadly dull that repetitious work can be. I lost interest early on and they also graduated me, this time with the degree of unemployed."

In a move that changed his life, Pat enlisted in the Marine Corps. At the time the Marine Corps was relatively small. Its 16,000 soldiers were smaller than the New York police force! There was one major difference between college, a job in a factory and the Marine Corps. You could not quit the Marines until the four-year enlistment was up!

After a year in San Diego, Pat was assigned to the Asiatic Station and boarded a troop ship heading for the Philippines. Pat said he thought the Philippines were in the Caribbean! One week after their arrival, the Japanese bombed Pearl Harbor to start World War II.

Hitchcock's unit, the 4th Marines, were assigned to defend the beaches of Corregidor. After five months of constant shelling, the island surrendered on May 6, 1942. Pat Hitchcock had become a prisoner of war. Rules for prisoners were quickly posted with this reminder at the bottom: "Prisoners who disobey rules will be severely shot to death."

At first the prisoners were held in a P.O.W. camp at Bilibio in Manilla. Water was plentiful, and they were fed rice three times a day. This soon ended when they were jammed into railroad freight cars and taken to the village of Cabanatuan. The next morning, they were force-marched twelve miles to Camp No. 3. Anyone who could not make the march was to be killed. Food was scarce and disease was rampant. Pat noted, "There was plenty of death to go around. The sad procession of pallbearers, carrying bodies on shutters, wending its way to the burying hole testified to that."

On July 17, 1944, the prisoners were forced into the holds of rusty cargo ships. With room only to stand and very little rice or water, conditions were beyond description. The trip to Japan took almost three weeks.

After arrival in Japan, the prisoners were moved to a prison camp in Oeyama where they remained until the war was over. Once again, conditions were brutal with scant clothing in bitter cold conditions. One guard, in particular, was especially cruel, beating the prisoners with a club.

When Pat Hitchcock was finally released, he weighed just under ninety-seven pounds. Suffering from vitamin deficiency, he was almost blind. After recovering from his years as a prisoner of war, he received an honorable discharge from the Marine Corps in August 1946. He was awarded the Silver Star, Bronze Star and two Purple Hearts.

Years later, several Japanese industries opened plants in

Jackson. It is customary to entertain their executives when they first visited. I teased Pat and asked him if he would like to play golf with them.

With a smile, he said, "I don't think that would be a good idea."

Years after the war, Pat had the opportunity to return to Japan on a business trip. Upon visiting the mine and factory where the prisoners had been held, he saw one of the former guards staring at him. His name was Watabe, the meanest of all the guards.

What a great story it would be if I could tell you they made peace and shook hands. Not so. Watabe quickly slipped away. For those two old soldiers, the war was not yet over.

Humorist Dave Gardner kept audiences laughing for many years in West Tennessee and around the country. His comedy album, "Rejoice Dear Hearts," made him a national celebrity.

Chapter 10

Two in the Spotlight

David Gardner, known as Brother Dave Gardner, was born in June 1926. Winston Conrad Martindale, known as "Wink," was born six and a half years later in 1933. Though there is little similarity between the two, it is unusual that both men were born in Jackson and had highly successful careers in the entertainment world.

After a one-semester term as a Southern Baptist ministerial student at Union University Brother Dave Gardner turned to music hoping to make a career as a drummer and occasional vocalist. In 1958 his recording of "White Silver Sands" was a top twenty hit.

It was his routine as a stand-up comedian with his Deep South accent and jokes that brought him to the attention of

Facebook video library
https://goo.gl/nKdgqC

RCA Records artist and producer Chet Atkins. The result was his comedy album "Rejoice Dear Hearts," which made him a national celebrity.

Gardner did six albums for RCA Victor and two for Capitol Records, plus others for lesser labels along with appearances on national television shows including *The Tonight Show*.

In 1962 he was arrested for marijuana possession, which curtailed his television visibility. In the mid-1960s, public tastes seemed to change, though Brother Dave's style of Southern humor did not. In the early '70s he did a brief prison stint for tax evasion. In his defense at the time, he told the judge, "I didn't know how much money I made, so I figured it was a fraud filling out one of those things."

In 1978 he had a role as a Southern preacher in a made-for-TV film, *Big Bob Johnson's Fantastic Speed Circus*. Five years later while working on a movie, he collapsed and died of a heart attack.

Brother Dave Gardner is remembered today for his Southern style of humor. Perhaps you have not heard of him. Even if you have, I doubt you knew he was from Jackson.

Remember him for his wit and unique way of expressing himself with sayings such as these:

"Folks used to pray to God for rain and now they call Washington."

"I like cigarettes — I'd smoke chains if I could light 'em."

"The difference between a Northern Baptist and a Southern Baptist was that a Northern Baptist said, 'There ain't no hell,' and a Southern Baptist said, 'The hell there ain't.'"

By contrast, "Wink" Martindale's career was more steady and predictable. Growing up in Jackson, he started his career as a disc jockey at age 17, spinning records on WPLI, a local station. After moving to WTJS, he was hired away for twice the salary to WDXI, Jackson's only other radio station. By this time his salary was $50 a week.

Martindale's first break into television came at WHBQ in Memphis while he was a student at Memphis State University, where he hosted *Mars Patrol*, a science fiction children's television show. In Memphis, he is best remembered for hosting the TV show *Teenage Dance Party*, where his friend Elvis Presley made an appearance.

In 1959 his rendition of the spoken word song "Deck of Cards" reached No. 7 on Billboard's Hot 100 chart. Four years later, the song peaked at No. 5 in the United Kingdom.

After graduating from college, he moved to California, where he hosted morning shows in Los Angeles for the next five years. In 1964 he hosted his first game show for NBC, *What's This Song?* Serving as a game show emcee was a perfect role for him, and the path he followed for the next thirty-four years.

Following *What's This Song?* his first major success was a new CBS game show, *Gambit*, which lasted four years. The emcee role for which Wink is best known is *Tic Tac Dough*, one of the most popular game shows ever produced. He was the emcee for seven years from 1978 to 1985.

From 1964 to 1996, he produced or emceed twelve different game shows.

On June 2, 2006, Martindale received a star on the Hollywood

Walk of Fame. Continuing to receive honors, he was one of the first inductees of the American TV Game Show Hall of Fame.

In 2012, Wink returned to radio as host of *The 100 Greatest Christmas Hits of All Time*. In 2014, he started his own YouTube channel called *Wink's Vault* featuring episodes from game shows. In 2016, he appeared on the daytime soap opera *The Bold and Beautiful* as a minister.

Seemingly ageless, Wink continues today on television and radio. He has come a long way since he started his career as a disc jockey on a radio station in Jackson.

Jackson native Wink Martindale left his mark on Hollywood and television game shows. He is best known as the emcee for *Tic Tac Dough*, one of the most popular game shows ever produced.

Colonel Harland Sanders gambled on chickens and his famous recipe — and won. Having grown up poor and struggled to make a living, he retired a millionaire.

Chapter 11

Twenty-Nine Chickens

Last week a young woman showed me her high school diploma. It had been a long journey for her with many setbacks. But now, she said with a big smile, "I move on to college."

Later I congratulated her father on his daughter's achievement. With a twinkle in his eye, he told me she reminded him of Colonel Sanders. Curious about the comparison, I asked him to explain it to me.

"Well," he said, "Harland Sanders grew up tough. His father died, and he wound up caring for his brother and sister. He had many jobs and lost most of them. By the time he was middle-aged, he was a failure in everything he tried. In desperation he went to a bank and borrowed enough money to

Facebook video library
https://goo.gl/nKdgqC

buy twenty-nine chickens. Taking them home, he cut them up, fried them and went door to door selling them. And that was the start of Kentucky Fried Chicken."

The next day I looked Colonel Sanders up. I never found the story about the twenty-nine chickens, but what I found was quite a story! And perhaps the biggest surprise was that he once lived and worked in Jackson, Tennessee!

Sanders was born in September 1890 on a small farm near Henryville, Indiana. He was the oldest of three children. His father worked the eighty-acre farm while his mother managed the children and prepared the meals. A devout Christian and strict parent, she warned the children about the evils of alcohol, tobacco, gambling and whistling on Sunday!

When he was five, his father died and his mother was forced to go to work in a tomato cannery. She was frequently gone for days at a time. At the age of five, Harland Sanders was the man of the house, taking care of and cooking for his younger siblings.

In 1902 his mother remarried and the family moved to Greenwood, Indiana. A year later, he dropped out of the seventh grade, saying, "Algebra's what run me off."

Because of disagreements with his new stepfather, Harland lived and worked on a nearby farm.

This move to a neighbor's farm and the work he did to pay for his room and board was his first real job. By the time he was forty, he had worked at fifteen different jobs. None of the jobs seemed to last very long so he moved from Indiana to Alabama to Tennessee and Kentucky.

In 1906, he enlisted in the army for a one-year commitment in Cuba. Following his discharge, he moved to Sheffield, Alabama, with the Southern Railway. After two months there, he moved to Jasper, Alabama, to work for the Northern Alabama Railroad. By 1909, he was working for the Norfolk and Western Railroad. His next job was with the Illinois Central Railroad in Jackson, Tennessee!

While he lived in Jackson, he studied law at night at the LaSalle Extension University. While he was working for the Illinois Central in Jackson, he got into a fight with another employee and lost his job.

During this time, he also sold life insurance, sold automobile tires, took a job for a year as a chamber of commerce secretary and established a ferry boat company on the Ohio River. Twice he was fired for fighting and once for insubordination. All of this happened in a ten-year period!

In 1924, entirely by chance, he met the general manager of Standard Oil of Kentucky, who asked him to run a service station in Nicholasville, Kentucky, which he did for six years until the station was closed due to the Great Depression.

In 1930 Shell offered Sanders a service station in North Corbin, Kentucky, rent free, in return for paying them a percentage of sales. In an adjacent area, he opened a restaurant serving chicken dishes, country ham and steaks. Lunch was fifty cents to a dollar, and supper was ten cents more.

Nine years later Sanders acquired a motel in Asheville, North Carolina, but once again bad luck caught up with him. When the Japanese attacked Pearl Harbor in December 1941, gas was rationed and the tourist business dried up, forcing him to close the motel.

In 1952 Sanders franchised his secret recipe for the first time to Pete Harmon of South Salt Lake, Utah, operator of the city's largest restaurant. Harmon's business tripled in the first year. As other restaurant owners heard of Harmon's success, they too joined in, paying four cents per chicken.

Deciding to pursue the franchise concept in earnest, he traveled across the country looking for suitable restaurants. Often sleeping in the back of his car, Sanders visited restaurants, offering to cook his chicken, and if workers liked it, he negotiated the franchise rights. Eventually restaurant owners began calling on him.

The franchise approach became highly successful; KFC was one of the first fast food chains to expand internationally by the mid-1960s.

In 1962, Sanders obtained a patent protecting his method of pressure-frying chicken. In 1963 he trademarked the phrase "It's Finger Licking Good." Sanders bragged that his gravy was so good, "It'll make you throw away the durn chicken and just eat the gravy."

By 1964, there were more than 600 KFC locations. Sanders was then seventy-three years old and feeling overwhelmed by the number of franchises. He sold the company to a group of investors for two million dollars. Even though he no longer owned the company, he remained as the image of the franchises, traveling 200,000 miles a year on behalf of the company.

After being recommissioned as a Kentucky colonel in 1950,

Sanders began to dress the part, growing a goatee and wearing a white suit and string tie.

In 1980, at the age of ninety, Colonel Harland Sanders died. It had been a remarkable career after years of false starts and failures. One simple fact remained that Colonel Harland Sanders knew how to cook chicken better than anyone else. From four cents a chicken to hundreds of franchises, it had been quite a run.

The book *Miss Minerva and William Green Hill* was first published in February 1909 and has since gone through more than fifty printings.

Chapter 12

Miss Minerva

Do you remember William Green Hill? If your age is less than seventy, I would bet that the name is unfamiliar to you. The book *Miss Minerva and William Green Hill* was first published in February 1909 and has since gone through more than fifty printings!

The author was Frances Boyd Calhoun, a schoolteacher in Covington, Tennessee.

The book successfully caught the infectious spirit of children, as much today as it did more than a century ago. The book is a timeless celebration of the freshness and sheer joy of childhood.

Frances Boyd Calhoun was born in Mecklenburg County, Virginia, on Christmas Day in 1867, just two years after the end of the Civil War. The family lived in North Carolina for

Facebook video library
https://goo.gl/nKdgqC

several years before moving to Covington in West Tennessee in 1880. After graduating from Tipton Female Seminary in 1880, she assisted her father in editing a local newspaper, sometimes publishing poetry there and in a Memphis newspaper.

For seven years she taught school in the Covington school system. In 1903 she married George Barret Calhoun, who died just one year later, leaving her a widow. Five years later she too died, being only forty-two.

Miss Minerva and William Green Hill was the only book that Frances Boyd Calhoun wrote before her untimely death. It came out just a few months after her death. She never knew anything about the success of the book or the delight and laughter of thousands of her readers.

At the time the book was written, there were very few publishers in the South. As a consequence, the book was published in Chicago. The manuscript was delivered to publishers Reilly and Britton in spring 1908, but the manuscript was set aside to be read at a more convenient time.

In Covington, Frances Boyd Calhoun waited for a response, but none was forthcoming. Finally in August, she sent a rhymed letter to the publisher.

"On the seventh of March, nineteen hundred and eight,
Mr. Reilly, I sent you my book,
And sure since that date for a letter from you
Each day I've continued to look.
Is it pigeon-holed now where the bookworm alone
May laugh and grow fat on each joke,

Where canker and rust will eat out the hearts
Of my dear little, quaint little folk?
Or, alas, has it vanished from all human ken,
The hard work of two long, long years?
With the public ne'er know of its merit and worth,
Its laughter, its sighs and its tears?
Or has it already been published in full,
And the 'steenth printing given it fame?
And instead of the title I gave it myself
Is it christened with some other name?
If naught has befallen it, may I still hope
You'll send my lost child back to me?
And I'll start it anew on its difficult path,
Please ship it at once C.O.D.
FRANCES CALHOUN
Covington, Tenn.

The publisher's response was immediate, and it was published the following February. Four months after it was published, Frances Calhoun died. She never knew of the little book's success or of the generations of people who have loved it. Today, I expect few people are aware of William Green Hill or Miss Minerva. The book faithfully reflects the dialect or the language of the time even if it is difficult for today's reader. In the book's first paragraph, William Green Hill, an orphan, is delivered to Miss Minerva. The bus driver (horse-drawn carriage) tries to explain why the little boy is sitting up on the driver's seat with him.

"T wan't no use fer ter try ter make him ride nowhars but jes'
up by me. He jes' 'fused an' 'fused an' 'sputed an' 'sputed; he jes'
tuck ter me f'om de minute he got off 'm de train an' sot eyes on
me; he am one easy chile ter git 'quainted wid; so, I jes' h'isted
him up by me. Here am his verlise, ma'am."

One item that is problematic is that some names of a hundred years ago are socially incorrect today, especially with African-Americans.

Though the book is about Covington, Tennessee, it could be about any similar sized-town in America a hundred years ago. William Green Hill is the story of a six-year-old orphan who came to live with his aunt, Miss Minerva, an old maid schoolteacher. Despite the fact that she has a suitor, "the Major," she turns her nose up at anything that wears pants. Her solution is to raise Billy, as he calls himself, as a girl. Billy is not a girl, but she will rear him as if he were, and he will be a splendid individual, a candidate for the ministry.

This sets the stage as Billy and his three playmates thwart her plans. Billy is Billy, and he plans to be nothing else. All things considered, William Green Hill is a six-year-old boy, full of life and mischief. But more than that, it is about the joy of childhood — a story for successive generations who, like Billy, were once six years old and all the world was new.

The Ames Plantation, located near Grand Junction, is the site of the National Field Trial Championships held each year in February. The National Bird Dog Museum is in Grand Junction.

Chapter 13

Ames Plantation

It all started with a small brown bird about the size of a meadowlark. Ruddy with a short, dark tail, the male has a white throat and a white brow stripe. You would recognize this bird by its distinctive call of "Bobwhite, Bobwhite."

When was the last time you saw a native Tennessee "Bobwhite" quail? They once lived all around us. If you grew up on a farm in West Tennessee, or even lived in a rural area, chances are a covey of quail lived in a thicket nearby. Chances are you heard their distinctive call early in the morning and late in the afternoon.

Quail were part of our environment long before whitetail deer were reintroduced in Tennessee. They were here before wild turkeys returned. Beavers, minks and otters have returned to our

Facebook video library
https://goo.gl/nKdgqC

wetlands. Coyotes and even mountain lions are now present. Who knows what could be next? West Tennessee once had black bears and elk. Our fields and woodlands, and the creatures who live there, continue to change.

One thing, however, that has changed dramatically is the land around us. No more do we have small fields and food plots. Agriculture and large machinery have changed the landscape.

Whether it is the increase of hawks or owls or numerous other predators, or the loss of habitat, our quail population has become a thing of the past. Perhaps one day they will return.

Coveys of quail, or "Bobwhites," are found along the edge of fields or nearby thickets. When flushed, they explode into the air like rockets. Generations of Southern people and their bird dogs have hunted quail once common throughout the South. To do so is a longstanding Southern tradition.

In 1901 Hobart Ames, a wealthy industrialist from North Easton, Massachusetts, purchased 18,567 acres in Fayette and Hardeman counties. He operated the plantation as a hunting preserve for "Bobwhite" quail and as a cotton plantation and livestock operation. The Ameses would come there in late December of each year and stay until late March. Hobart Ames died in 1945 and his wife, Julia, died five years later in 1950.

Prior to her death, Mrs. Ames established a foundation to operate under the ownership of the trustees of the foundation to benefit the University of Tennessee and to provide grounds and support for the national championships for field trialing bird dogs. The plantation has about 12,000 acres of forest, 2,000 acres of row crops, and maintains seven hundred cattle and forty horses.

Because of quail, the Ames Plantation continues to thrive today. If it had not been for quail, the Ameses would never have come south to buy the land.

The plantation is near the town of Grand Junction. The little town was established in 1848, fifty-three years before Hobart Ames came south to Tennessee. It sits at the junction of the Memphis and Charleston Railroad and the Mississippi Central Railroad, thus the name of Grand Junction. Union soldiers occupied the town for three years during the Civil War, and in 1878 yellow fever killed half of the town's population. Fewer than three hundred people live there today.

West Tennessee has a rich hunting dog heritage. The area is recognized as the birthplace of America's pointing dog field trials and home of the century-old National Field Trial Championships.

The National Bird Dog Museum is located in Grand Junction and the National Field Trial Championships are held at the Ames Plantation each year beginning on the second or third Monday of February. Running on some six thousand acres, the trials last over a two-week period with several thousand people in attendance. The event has been run on the Ames Plantation since 1915.

Because of that little brown bird, our native "Bobwhite" quail, the Ameses came south and built the Ames Plantation. And, because of the field trials, the Bird Dog Museum is located in Grand Junction.

Modern farming practices, all across the South, have greatly reduced habitat necessary to sustain quail populations. However, the "Bobwhite" is still king at the Ames Plantation and will be for years to come.

Jesse Hill Ford was renowned for his book *The Liberation of Lord Byron Jones*. He also penned the novel *Mountains of Gilead*.

Chapter 14

Jesse Hill Ford

Jesse Hill Ford was born in Troy, Alabama, on December 28, 1928. When his father took a job with Upjohn Pharmaceutical Company, the family moved to Nashville.

After attending Montgomery Bell Academy, Ford enrolled at Vanderbilt University in 1947. When he graduated in 1951, he entered the Navy as an ensign and served in Korea for two years. After leaving the service, he enrolled at the University of Florida where he earned a master's degree.

When he finished his education, he worked in public relations for the Tennessee Medical Association for two years and then for the American Medical Association for seven months. In 1957 he resigned to write full time, moving to Humboldt, Tennessee, his wife's hometown.

Facebook video library
https://goo.gl/nKdgqC

Two years later he sold his first short story to *Atlantic Monthly*. The story won the magazine's Atlantic First award. His play, *The Conversion of Buster Drumwright*, was aired by CBS Television Workshop in 1960. The following year, after publishing his first novel, he won a Fulbright Scholarship to study and write in Norway.

When he returned to West Tennessee, he began working on a new novel, *The Liberation of Lord Byron Jones*, published by Atlantic-Little Brown in 1965. Although he wrote dozens of short stories and several screenplays, it was this novel that established his reputation. The book was the sort of success that every writer dreams of. It was a Book of the Month Club selection and also earned him a Guggenheim Fellowship for fiction writing. Not only did it make him famous, it made him rich.

In 1970 the book was made into a William Wyler movie starring Lee J. Cobb, Roscoe Lee Browne, Lola Falana and Anthony Zerbe, which gave it even wider circulation. The book is about a prosperous black undertaker who seems determined to obtain a dignified divorce from his young wife, who has been cheating on him. To do so, he names a white policeman as her lover. When the policeman learns of the plot, he shoots and kills the undertaker.

The novel did not make Ford popular with his neighbors and friends who knew that the story was based on actual events and real people. It might have been acceptable in a large city like Memphis or Nashville, but not in Humboldt where everybody knew everything and everybody.

In 1969 Ford published his third novel, *The Feast of St.*

Barnabas. Like its predecessor, this book also dealt with racial conflict. This time Ford and his family began receiving calls and threats. The situation deteriorated when black players were barred from the high school football team at the time when the town's school system was being integrated. Ford's son was the captain of the football team, and he too began receiving threats.

On the night of November 16, 1970, a young African-American soldier, Private George Henry Doaks Jr., drove up Ford's driveway and pulled off to the side of the road. With him was a sixteen-year-old African-American girl. Of all the places he could have chosen to park, this was the most unfortunate.

Jesse Hill Ford testified he was afraid the occupants of the car intended to harm his son Charles when he came home. Hoping to frighten the people in the car, according to his testimony, he fired two shots from a bolt-action .30-06 rifle, the second of which killed Private Doaks.

The following year Ford was charged with murdering the young soldier. The trial achieved national attention with coverage in Chicago and New York newspapers. Though he was found not guilty, it reminded many readers of the type of Southern justice described in his novels.

Though he continued to write, most people felt he never recovered from the trial. Four years after the trial he published his last novel, *The Raider*, which is similar in many ways to the exploits of Confederate General Nathan Bedford Forrest.

On May 31, 1996, after successful open-heart surgery, Ford became depressed and took his own life. He was sixty-seven.

Father Christmases, created by Myrtle Rose Emerson of Fruitvale, are nationally known.

Chapter 15

Fruitvale

Fruitvale is a small, unincorporated community in Crockett County, Tennessee. Less than thirty people live there today. At first it was known as Jackson Hollow, named for one of the early settlers. In the 1850s, the Mobile and Ohio Railroad was built through the area.

The town began to be known as "The Switch" when a railroad switch and siding were constructed there. Legend has it that the name was changed to Fruitvale at the suggestion of a hobo coming through the area. "Fruit" came from the amount of fruit and vegetables being shipped north on the railroad and "vale" came from its location on a small, level space between Bells and Gadsden, both of which sat on low hills.

Large amounts of strawberries, sweet potatoes, cabbage,

Facebook video library
https://goo.gl/nKdgqC

tomatoes and anything else that could be grown in bulk soon ended up in homes and restaurants far away. J.O. Boyd acted as the "middle man" buying and selling almost anything — hardware, groceries, dry goods, fertilizer, coal and appliances. Several of his warehouses were full of merchandise. He bought produce — cabbage, tomatoes, berries, beans and large amounts of sweet potatoes — and shipped them north on the railroads. The amount of produce leaving Fruitvale was so large it would have provided seasonal employment for most of the town. At the peak of the growing season, as many as eight railroad cars of green tomatoes were shipped daily.

Hardwood timber was also cut and shipped. The fruit and vegetables were shipped on ice, which had to be bought in Brownsville and brought on wagons thirteen miles back to Fruitvale.

In 1893 a post office was established. Several years later, in 1903, a business directory listed a blacksmith shop, a sawmill and several stores. Two brothers, J.O. "Ollie" and Oscar Boyd, opened a grocery store in 1906.

The train would come through Fruitvale every day at 10:45 a.m. and 6 p.m. Residents said they could set their watches by when the train arrived and left. When the train conductor called, "All aboard," the children thought he was saying, "Ollie Boyd," the owner of the store.

There were only two cars in the area in the 1920s! One of the cars was owned by Zab Williams. In addition to a car, he owned the only threshing machine. When it came time to harvest the wheat, all the men in the surrounding area would follow the machine and help harvest the wheat from one farm to the next. When the day was over, the lady of the farm where they were working would provide supper, usually fried chicken and fruit cobbler. Another resource for the people of the area who raised domestic geese were the goose feathers. The geese were killed, cleaned and shipped north while the feathers were used to make pillows to be sold to passengers on the trains.

In the early 1900s, a large wooden fruit shed was built adjacent to the railroad siding. Train cars could be parked adjacent to the shed for loading crates of fruits and vegetables.

In 1920 Fruitvale had about 260 residents. However, the population began to decline after World War II. In 1993, the Fruitvale post office served only thirty customers. At the time, it was considered to be the smallest post office in Tennessee. As the little town grew even smaller, the post office closed in 2010.

Sadly enough, Fruitvale no longer exists as a town. And yet it does exist in a different and even better way! In 2012 the Fruitvale Historic District was listed on the National Register of Historic Places. It includes two acres of land and nine buildings, the blacksmith shop, a bunkhouse, two sheds, a barn, a seed preparation house and scale and two stores. The train still goes by the seed barn but no longer stops.

Myrtle Rose Leggett Emerson lives nearby. Her roots go back to the early settlers. If you want to visit the Fruitvale general store, she has the key. Built in 1917, the store was first named J.O. Boyd General Merchandise. Closed more than twenty years ago, it is filled with merchandise of years gone by.

In the late 1980s, Myrtle Rose began making "Father

Christmases." They were made at first from two-liter Coke bottles, but she soon began making larger ones, built with wooden inserts, wire arms and a face molded from papier mache and hand-painted. The figures are clothed in antique quilts with pheasant feathers, dried okra, broom straw and, as she puts it, "whatever I find when I wander in the woods."

Myrtle Rose is quick to point out, "They are not Santa Claus, but Father Christmases." Found in homes throughout the Mid-South, and as far away as Texas and Colorado, they bring back memories of holiday seasons of long ago.

The area around Fruitvale still produces large amounts of fruits and vegetables. Unlike the past, most of what is grown in West Tennessee remains in West Tennessee. Yet the little village remains, much as it was decades ago. Life was slower then, and with the pace we now go, perhaps it was better!

Henry Rutherford spent three months of 1785 establishing on the first bluff of the Forked Deer "Key Corner" from which point he began his surveys. On a leaning sycamore tree on the south bank of the river, he carved "HR" with a large key above it to indicate it as the key to all his Forked Deer surveys.

Chapter 16

The Key to It All

In 1783, thirty-five years prior to the treaty with the Chickasaw Indians, the state of North Carolina opened a land office for the purpose of selling two and a half million acres of land in what is now Tennessee. Tennessee would not come into the Union until 1796.

Demand was so high that little could be accomplished for the first three days until a system of casting lots was set up to see who could go first. Prices were as low as 12½ cents an acre. Any citizen of North Carolina could purchase up to five thousand acres of land. With so much excitement, it is little wonder the new land was called "The Promised Land" or "The Garden of Eden."

Even though the real landowners, the Chickasaw Indians, had no intention of selling even one acre of land, the North Carolina

Facebook video library
https://goo.gl/nKdgqC

legislature sent surveyors to locate and survey the purchases.

James Robertson, Henry Rutherford and Edward Harris were selected to go into the district and survey the lands. Henry Rutherford, son of General Griffith Rutherford, after whom Rutherford County was named, was born in Rowan County, North Carolina, in August 1762. The area was called the "Western District." In June 1785, they descended the Cumberland, the Ohio and the Mississippi to the mouth of a small river that emptied into the Mississippi from the east. The Indian name for this river was Okeena, but the surveyors soon changed the name to Forked Deer. A large deer with unusual horns was killed nearby, thus the name Forked Deer, which continues to the present.

Rutherford spent three months establishing on the first bluff of the Forked Deer "Key Corner" from which point he began his surveys. On a leaning sycamore tree on the south bank of the river, he carved "HR" with a large key above it to indicate it as the key to all his Forked Deer surveys. This was the beginning corner for four of his locations. The first was for 3,000 acres in the name of Griffith Rutherford, his father. During Henry Rutherford's visit to West Tennessee, he located more than 365,000 acres of land of which 13,500 acres were for himself.

Rutherford was in West Tennessee for three months. When food ran low, the party lived on deer, elk, bears and wild turkeys, which they found in abundance. The heavy growth of vines was a great inconvenience, for they were so dense that the dragging of the survey chains left a trail. Because of concerns that the Chickasaw Indians would resent their presence, the group camped a half mile away each night. Yet when the group returned home, they reported they had not even seen an Indian!

Finally in 1818, commissioners were appointed to negotiate a treaty with the Indians. General Andrew Jackson of Tennessee and Isaac Shelby of Kentucky began the negotiations. When the Chickasaws told Jackson they had "no lands either to exchange or sell," he sent back word that "the citizens had been kept out of possession of this land for thirty-odd years and individuals who had bought and paid for it demanded possession of it, and their father the President will be compelled to give it to them."

After twenty days of arguments and negotiations, the Jackson-Shelby Treaty was finalized whereby the Indians were to receive $300,000 payable in fifteen installments.

Rutherford had returned to West Tennessee in 1811 and 1816 to refresh his memory of his surveys. When the treaty was signed, he helped owners identify their land grants for a percentage of the land. He received 600 acres for each 5,000 acres he had surveyed.

Reports that much of the new land was well-suited for growing cotton set the land speculators "on fire." By 1820, there were one hundred surveyors in the territory. "Western District fever" was nearly as bad as that of the California Gold Rush. The settlement of West Tennessee had begun.

Henry Rutherford was the first to lead a group of pioneers back to Key Corner and the old sycamore tree where his survey had started so many years earlier. Rutherford settled on a tract about two miles east of Key Corner. He lived there with his family until he died in 1847, more than sixty years after his survey team first set foot there. He is buried nearby and perhaps somewhere close at hand, his initials are still on that tree.

Over a period of seven months, masked men on horseback committed more than 120 crimes ranging from arson to murder because of a legal fight over the fishing rights to Reelfoot Lake.

Chapter 17

Night Riders of Reelfoot

Halloween can be a scary time, a time when spooks and witches and all sorts of creatures appear. It is a night when good people, gentle people, put on masks, and it seems to change them into something bad, something that frightens us. Watch a small child's reaction to a person with a mask on; they don't like it. What if you saw a group of masked men, and it wasn't Halloween? What if they were on horses and it was the middle of the night? And what if they were coming to hurt you? You would be frightened as the people of Reelfoot Lake once were.

Reelfoot Lake is located in the northwest corner of Tennessee in Lake and Obion counties. The lake was created by a series of earthquakes in 1811-1812, among the most intense the United States has ever known. The Mississippi River tore through its

Facebook video library
https://goo.gl/nKdgqC

banks north of Tiptonville. Eyewitnesses reported that it ran backward for several days, creating a 25,000-acre lake some twenty miles long and two to seven miles wide.

Despite its natural beauty, the area and its people are different from other areas in West Tennessee. The land around the lake and the quality of the soil do not lend themselves to large farms or plantations. Many of the families derived their income from fishing on the lake or subsistence farming on the edge of Reelfoot Lake.

Although claims on the land existed prior to the earthquake that created the lake, the local population regarded the lake as public domain. It was their lake, and had been so for generations, despite the fact that someone else held the title to it.

Tempers escalated to a fever pitch when the West Tennessee Land Company purchased the land with the intention of controlling the fishing rights as well as draining a portion of the lake and converting it to land to grow cotton. Over a period of seven months, masked men on horseback committed more than 120 crimes ranging from arson to murder. Many men and women were savagely beaten, and some were run out of the area, or left fearing for their safety.

It is probable that no more than twenty men participated willingly in the crimes. However, ten to fifteen times that number joined in because of intimidation and fear. Though fishing rights and control of the lake were the catalysts, a large portion of the crimes had nothing to do with Reelfoot Lake. Control of the lake was simply an excuse for the crimes they committed. For a seven-month period, a blanket of fear covered the entire western side of Obion County and part of Fulton County, Kentucky.

The Night Riders used "seven wonders" as one of their passwords with the countersign being "I wonder." The Riders divided themselves into the Lower and Upper Lake gangs. The Lower Lake Gang lived around Samburg and the Upper Lake Gang lived around Walnut Log.

The Riders wore masks and gowns or capes. The masks were fashioned from meal sacks and secured by string. A stripe of white paint circled the slits for eyes and mouth.

For seven months — from April to October 1908 — the Reelfoot region suffered in a reign of terror and violence. Immoral women received whippings. Husbands were whipped for failing to provide support to their families. The Riders' purpose seemed to be to control the entire community in which they lived and to be in themselves the controlling government.

During the seven months of their reign, the Night Riders gained notoriety for four crimes they committed. The first was burning the fishing docks of J.C. Burdick, who controlled the largest wholesale fish business on the lake. Because he had to pay the land company an annual fee, Burdick had reduced the payments to the fishermen. On the evening of April 11, a crowd of fifty fishermen burned his docks. Burdick abandoned his Reelfoot Lake property and moved to Union City. Reactions from the sheriff and police were negligible.

Later that month twelve masked men rode into Lake County to "administer a lesson" to George Wynne, who had made unkind remarks about the Night Riders. The aged, hunchbacked farmer was bent barebacked over a stump and whipped with a thorn bush. Months later, Wynne died as a result of the injuries he received.

In October, the Riders rode north into Brownsville, Kentucky, where they attacked Dave Walker, a black farmer whom they considered as arrogant. Walker attempted to defend himself but was shot to death when his cabin was set on fire. His wife, a baby and a twelve-year-old daughter also were killed, and three other children were wounded but survived.

On October 14, the West Tennessee Land Company received confirmation of its exclusive ownership of the lake, which prohibited the fishermen or anyone else from profiting on the lake without its permission. This rekindled the Night Riders' determination to "save the lake."

On October 19, two prominent attorneys from Trenton, Robert Z. Taylor and Quentin Rankin, came to the lake to help negotiate a lease on Grassy Island and Caney Ridge, part of the land owned by West Tennessee Land Company. Both attorneys were employed by the land company. After surveying the tracts to be leased, Rankin and Taylor returned to P.C. Ward's hotel for supper and a night's lodging.

Just after eleven o'clock, thirty-five Night Riders forced their way into the hotel and ordered the two attorneys to get dressed and come with them. Rankin and Taylor were then forced to accompany the group about a quarter of a mile to a slough that led into the lake.

Quentin Rankin at age thirty-nine was the younger of the two attorneys. Considered by many to be one of the brightest attorneys in Tennessee, he was a graduate of Vanderbilt

University. When asked directly to reopen the lake to free public fishing, he responded, "I couldn't possibly do that."

When a noose was placed around Rankin's neck, one Rider shouted, "Give him time to pray," to which Rankin responded, "Gentlemen, I've already tended to that."

After refusing a compromise on the fishing question, a blast from a shotgun ended his life.

As the Night Riders debated Taylor's fate, he dove into the slough as a rain of shots followed him. Taylor, the older of the two attorneys, was sixty-three but in very good shape. A former Confederate officer, he had ridden with Nathan Bedford Forrest in the Civil War.

Taylor hid behind a sunken log and remained there for more than an hour until the horsemen departed. He then began an epic journey that lasted two days and covered more than twenty-five miles of harsh terrain. On the morning of the twenty-first, he staggered out of the woods where a farmer found him and carried him to safety.

The story of the arrest and trial of the Night Riders is a tale in itself. Governor Malcolm Patterson took charge and arrived at the lake with the Tennessee National Guard. By the end of October, nearly one hundred suspects were being held in a makeshift camp. Eventually, six of the defendants were found guilty and sentenced to death by hanging. The Tennessee Supreme Court overturned their conviction in 1909.

The seven-month period of the Night Riders' reign of terror was over. The sound of hoof beats in the night would be heard no more. The Night Riders lost the fight, or did they? Public opinion so favored the people of Reelfoot Lake that in 1914, the state of Tennessee acquired title to the lake, ending the threat of private ownership.

Today, Reelfoot is a major attraction for people who come there to hunt or to fish. With the many festivals, cypress trees and bald eagles, the lake is as popular as ever. And yet in some ways Reelfoot seems to hold onto the past. Duck blinds mysteriously burn up or simply disappear. The spot where Quentin Rankin lost his life is much the same as it was in 1908. Though the dark days of the Night Riders are a thing of the past, it is easy to imagine the terror that surrounded them. If you are at Reelfoot on a night in October, listen closely. You may hear the sound of mounted horsemen coming toward you. Perhaps it is your imagination. Or is it?

Ellis Kinder was the only Jackson baseball player to make it to the major leagues. After the close of the 1949 season, Kinder was named the American League pitcher of the year.

Chapter 18

Ellis Kinder, 'Old Folks'

Ellis Raymond Kinder was born in July 1914 in Atkins, Arkansas, near Russellville. Part of a large family, Ellis had three brothers and numerous sisters. His father was a farmer raising cotton and corn. With meager income, it was a constant struggle to support them.

By the time he was ten years old, Ellis helped to support the family. After completing the eighth grade, Ellis told school "goodbye" and went to work. In 1937, when he was twenty-three, both of his parents died, and he was obliged to support three of his siblings as well as his own wife and children.

That year, when he was offered a job to pitch for the Jackson Generals (Tennessee) in the Class D Kitty League, he said he could not afford to work four months at $75 a month and feed

Facebook video library
https://goo.gl/nKdgqC

a family. In 1938, he was again offered a spot in the Generals roster but turned it down again.

In 1939, for the third straight year, he was offered a job to pitch for Jackson. This time his boss told him to play baseball and promised to hold his job for him when the season was over.

Pitching full time for the Generals, Kinder had a record of seventeen wins and twelve losses with an average of 3.59 runs allowed per game.

In 1940 again pitching for Jackson, he won twenty-one games with only nine losses leading the league in strikeouts. He was twenty-six years old when the season ended.

Despite Kinder's advanced age, the New York Yankees were sufficiently impressed to purchase his option for five thousand dollars and sent him to Birmingham of the Southern Association. After six games, the Yankees released him, and he returned to Jackson where his family now lived.

In 1942, Kinder pitched for Jackson, Mississippi, and for Memphis before returning to Jackson, Tennessee, where he took a better-paying job as a pipefitter with the Illinois Central Railroad and gave up his baseball career. As much as he loved baseball, he needed the money for his family.

In 1944, baseball was short of quality pitchers with World War II in full swing. As a result, Memphis manager Doc Protho offered Kinder a contract to return to Memphis. When Protho told Ellis, "I need pitchers," Kinder responded, "The Illinois Central needs pipefitters!" Two days later, Protho substantially increased the offer, and Ellis Kinder put his uniform on once more.

Kinder was the star of the 1944 Memphis team and was the best pitcher in the Southern Association with a record of nineteen wins and only six losses. His teammate Pete Gray was the most famous player on the team with a batting average of .333 despite not having a right arm! Pete Gray is a story himself. Not only did he have a high batting average, he stole sixty-eight bases that year. A left fielder, Gray could catch the ball in his glove and in one motion transfer the ball to his good hand and throw it back.

After the season, both Ellis Kinder and Pete Gray were called up to the St. Louis Browns. They had made it to the big leagues. Or so it seemed! Pete Gray did play a full season with the Browns, but Ellis got a call from the U.S. Navy. The uniform he put on was not the one he anticipated.

Kinder finally got to the "big leagues" in 1946. He was nearly thirty-two years old, making him one of the oldest rookies to be a major leaguer! After two mediocre seasons with the lowly Browns, Kinder was traded to the Boston Red Sox in November 1947.

When Ellis reported to the Red Sox the following year, his reputation as a hard drinker and woman-chaser preceded him. And yet, no matter how drunk he got, or how little sleep he got, he was always ready to play the next day. Nearing his thirty-fourth birthday, he was at an age when many athletes are thinking about retiring. Ellis was just getting started. He was as competitive as players in their mid-twenties.

Off to a slow start because of an injury to his right arm, he was well by midsummer and in fine form, winning ten of his last seventeen starts. For the Red Sox, it was also a good year despite the fact they lost the pennant to the Cleveland Indians on the last game of the season.

Once again, in 1949, Boston had the chance to win the pennant. As the season drew to a close, the Red Sox and the Yankees had identical records. The winner of the American League pennant would be decided in the final game. Kinder, at the time, was the best pitcher in baseball with a record of twenty-three wins and only five losses. He was scheduled to pitch the final game.

Thinking a drink or two would steady his nerves, two of the Red Sox players asked Arthur Richmond, a New York sports writer, to take Ellis out and get him drunk. And they proceeded to do that! Richmond helped Ellis to bed when they got back to the hotel. It was 4:30 a.m.! A few hours later, Kinder pitched the game of his life, giving up only one run in eight innings before being taken out for a pinch hitter. Once again, the Red Sox lost 5-3. Even today, Red Sox fans debate the decision to take Ellis out of the game. After the close of the season, Kinder was named the American League pitcher of the year.

In the 1950 season, the Red Sox converted Ellis from a starting pitcher to a relief pitcher, feeling he would be better utilized in that way. Though he was thirty-six years old, it seemed like his career was just beginning. In 1951, Kinder pitched in sixty-three games, more than any other pitcher in the league. He was honored that year as the team's Most Valuable Player.

In 1953, at the age of thirty-nine, he broke the league's record for most games pitched in a single season. His earned run average was a microscopic low of 1.85! When the manager, Lou Boudreau signaled for Ellis to come in to pitch, he would put his hand on his head, signifying a crown for the king of relief pitchers!

When he turned forty, the following year he pitched in forty-eight games but was sidelined for part of the season with a throat infection and pneumonia. He had become quite famous for his success at such an advanced age, earning him the nickname of "Old Folks."

In December 1955, Boston sold Ellis to the St. Louis Cardinals. He had been part of the Red Sox organization for eight wonderful years. And yet, he was past the age when most players have long since retired.

At a farewell dinner in his honor, Ellis said, "Baseball's been very good to me. I've had a lot of thrills, and tonight is one of the biggest." After a short period with St. Louis, "Old Folks" called it quits, retired from baseball and returned to Jackson.

Though he was born in Arkansas, Jackson, Tennessee, was home for Ellis Kinder. He came here first to play baseball for the Jackson Generals. He worked here as a pipefitter for the Illinois Central Railroad. And as a major league pitcher, he came home when the season was over. Even today, more than sixty years after his retirement, Ellis Kinder is one of the greatest Red Sox pitchers of all time.

In poor health, he went through open-heart surgery in a Memphis hospital. Jackson did not offer open-heart surgery then. Two days after the surgery, on October 16, 1968, Kinder died of complications. Jackson's all-time best baseball player was only fifty-four. He is buried in Jackson at Highland Memorial Gardens.

Ray Blanton was a controversial figure in Tennessee politics. He served three terms in the U.S. House of Representatives, then was elected governor of Tennessee from 1975-1979.

Chapter 19

Ray Blanton: The Road to Nashville

The Shiloh Methodist Church is located within Shiloh National Military Park. Shiloh means "Place of Peace," but Shiloh is anything but that. Adjacent to the church is a Methodist cemetery, surrounded by Civil War monuments and cannons. In the middle of the cemetery is a large obelisk. It marks the grave of Leonard Ray Blanton, the forty-fourth governor of the state of Tennessee. Perhaps it is fitting that he is buried in a place where fighting swirled all around him.

Ray Blanton came up tough. Shorty Freeland, Blanton's patronage aide, described it this way: "You can't understand the way he is unless you know where he came from. He's an outsider. He's not part of the political establishment in this state. Ray Blanton stands for the people who never had a voice

Facebook video library
https://goo.gl/nKdgqC

because he was one of them. He grew up in a sharecropper's shack during the Depression. You don't have any idea what that was like. The cracks in the walls were so wide you could throw a rat through them."

Ray Blanton was born near the small settlement of New Hope in rural Hardin County. The house was isolated from neighbors in the middle of a large cotton field that backed up to Shiloh Park. He made his first crop at age eleven, walking behind a one-row plow and a pair of mules.

His first formal schooling was in a Hardin County grammar school classroom heated by a potbellied stove. Ray used to tell a story of the family pulling up a loose board on the front porch, reaching down and robbing the hens of their eggs. Somewhat as a surprise, Ray was a better than average student by the time he entered Shiloh High School, where he received a Danforth Foundation Award for outstanding scholarship.

Following high school, Ray enrolled at the University of Tennessee. In 1949, he returned home long enough to marry his high school sweetheart, Betty Littlefield. He graduated in 1951 with a degree in agriculture.

Despite his college degree, in many ways he was unchanged. He often struggled with his grammar — a reflection of his education in rural West Tennessee where the emphasis was often more on getting the crops in than on learning the rules of grammar.

After graduating from the University of Tennessee, Ray and his wife Betty moved to Mooresville, Indiana, where Ray took a job teaching school. During the time Ray and Betty lived in

Mooresville, Ray contracted polio and was in the hospital for several months. He suffered no permanent effects, but the illness had given him time to think about what the future held for him.

While Ray was teaching school in Indiana, the Blanton family had moved to Adamsville, the county seat of McNairy County. With a $10,000 bank loan, his father Leonard and brother Gene started a road-building company called B&B Construction Company. Rather than continuing to teach, Ray decided to return home and join the family business. As a further incentive to come home, Ray's father had been elected mayor of Adamsville. The future looked promising.

B&B specialized in concrete bridge and culvert work, and the man who would one day be governor found himself doing everything from rolling a wheelbarrow to operating bulldozers and draglines. After learning the business, Ray and brother Gene became onsite foremen for roadwork the company did with county, state and federal governments. For ten years, Ray lived with his family in a mobile home as they moved from one job site to another. During this time period, Betty and Ray had two children.

In those days, Tennessee had its own standards of road building and construction. Contractors who "didn't play the game" rarely won contracts. Bid rigging was common. For the Blanton brothers, it was a way of life, and they learned it well. Gene Blanton would one day be convicted of bid rigging on state road contracts, and a reporter wrote that he said, "When in Rome, do as the Romans do."

In the mid-1960s, Ray Blanton was beginning to think

about a new career. He had been living in a trailer for ten years, dragging his family from one job site to the next. The Blantons moved back to Adamsville when an opportunity presented itself. In 1964, the incumbent state representative did not stand for re-election. Ray won the Democratic position unopposed, and in the general election, there was no Republican candidate. Ray Blanton was on his way to Nashville!

When Ray Blanton arrived in Nashville as a freshman representative, it was the beginning of his fifteen-year political career. His two years in Nashville were undistinguished. His seat was in the back of the chamber, and he rarely rose to address his colleagues. Old newspaper stories indicate he often wore dark glasses after a night on the town. It was during this two-year period that he witnessed the absolute power of Governor Frank Clement. This would continue until 1970 when Winfield Dunn ended fifty years of Democratic control of the governor's office.

Following his two years in Nashville, Ray surprised everyone with an announcement that he intended to run for Congress. Tennessee's Seventh District was represented at the time by Democrat Tom Murray, the long-serving dean of the Tennessee delegation. He had held that office for twenty-four years. More than a congressman, he was an institution.

Blanton went town by town into every store and business he could find. Traveling in a private bus with his family, his message was simple: "I'm Ray Blanton, and I'm running for Congress."

The result was a shocking upset. Blanton defeated Murray by just over 300 votes! He had defeated a Tennessee legend.

Ray's opponent in the general election was Julius Hurst, superintendent of schools in McNairy County and chairman of the state Republican Party. With a name like Hurst and all of the support from "the Hurst Nation," he would be hard to beat. When the votes were counted, Ray had won by more than 2,000 votes. At the age of thirty-seven, he was headed to Washington!

Blanton represented Tennessee's Seventh Congressional District for six years. His voting record during those years reflects the rural conservative attitudes of his constituents. Key concerns were industrial development for rural areas, forced busing, and law and order.

Tennessee lost a congressional district after the 1970 census. Most of Blanton's territory was merged into the neighboring Eighth District, represented by the popular Ed Jones. Rather than trying to run against Jones, Blanton elected to run against the Republican incumbent Howard Baker.

Baker aligned himself with President Richard Nixon. Blanton, on the other hand, tried to distance himself from the head of the Democratic Party, George McGovern. Despite all of Blanton's efforts, Baker won by over 300,000 votes. Still, Blanton had made a strong campaign crossing back and forth, shaking hands throughout the Volunteer State. It would soon pay off for him.

In many ways, 1974 was the perfect year for Ray Blanton to run for governor. Watergate had devastated the Republicans. Nixon's resignation came just three months before the election, and his pardon by President Gerald Ford gave Democrats all the material they needed.

"This is the Democratic year," proclaimed Representative

Joe Evins, dean of the state congressional delegation. "The time has come for all you Democrats to come home to the faith of your fathers. And to those who may have sinned and voted Republican, tell them to come back."

Blanton won a twelve-person Democratic primary with just 23 percent of the vote. His opponents included East Tennessee banker Jake Butcher and former Senator Ross Bass.

His opponent in the general election was Lamar Alexander, who had worked in the Nixon White House for eighteen months. Though Alexander's duties had kept him far removed from Watergate, Blanton ripped him daily for his ties to Nixon and Watergate.

Blanton said, "Tennessee didn't want a Nixon-trained, Vanderbilt-educated, big city, young Republican lawyer, born with a silver spoon in his mouth, to control the reins of power in their state. They wanted one of their own — a man of the soil who had pulled himself up from the depths of poverty by the strength of his own will to become a successful businessman, a congressman and now a candidate for governor."

The message worked. When the returns were in, Blanton had beaten Lamar Alexander by 120,000 votes!

The inauguration of Leonard Ray Blanton marked the end of a long, hard road from a sharecropper's cabin that ended in the Tennessee state capital. More than ten thousand people waited in the rain and high winds to see their new governor inaugurated. As the weather worsened, the ceremony was eventually moved inside the War Memorial Auditorium. The Nashville Banner reported: "Several of the spectators compared the joyous crowds with the Tennesseans who went to Washington for the inauguration of President Andrew Jackson."

An East Tennessee Democrat responded, "We've been out four years, and we sure don't mind standing in line for the man who got us back in." The first order of business in the governor's office was to take down the portrait of Abraham Lincoln and replace it with Andrew Jackson.

Most stories about the Blanton years focus on the pardons of fifty-two state prisoners and the liquor license scandals for which he was convicted and served twenty-two months in prison. I have chosen to write about the early years. From an improbable background, and always as an underdog, he defeated Tom Murray, Jake Butcher and Lamar Alexander.

Among the positive things accomplished during Blanton's term as governor was the extensive recruiting of foreign industrial prospects. He made several trips to Africa, the Middle East, Japan and Europe to bring business to Tennessee. He elevated the state's Office of Tourism to a cabinet-level department, the first governor in the nation to do so.

I am a frequent visitor at Shiloh. When I drive by Shiloh Church, I see Ray's monument and remember when I first met Ray one day in Adamsville when his banker, Coleman Smith, introduced me to him. In later years, when he lived in Jackson, our paths would frequently cross. As a historian, I prefer to remember him in the good times as he began the road to being the forty-fourth governor of the state of Tennessee.

From 1970 to 1977, Norbert Putnam played bass in 120 songs with Elvis Presley. Outside of the years Norbert played with Elvis, he is best known for his production of Jimmy Buffett, who had such songs as "Margaritaville," "Cheeseburger in Paradise" and "Changes in Latitude" among the albums they produced. Other artists he produced included Dave Loggins, Dan Fogelberg and Kris Kristofferson.

Chapter 20

Norbert Putnam, Musician and Producer

You never know what or who you might meet in a bank lobby. This was especially true for me one day while waiting in a line to make a deposit, when I realized the customer in front of me was a dog!

The dog, a large black standard poodle, had her back feet on the ground and her front paws on the teller window. The teller, seeing me waiting, said, "Mr. Alexander, this is Sofie Putnam." Sofie, who was enjoying a handful of "doggie treats," stopped chewing and looked at me. I was unsure whether to shake hands or run. A few minutes later, I met Sofie's owners, Norbert and Sheryl Putnam. And though I met Norbert many times when he lived in Jackson, I always remembered that first day in the bank.

In the weeks that followed, stories of Norbert's legendary

Facebook video library
https://goo.gl/nKdgqC

past began to unfold. When I looked him up on the internet, it was hard to believe what I found. When names like Elvis Presley, Jimmy Buffett, Ray Charles and many others appeared, we began to realize who was living on 28 Northwood Avenue, right across the street from my son and in a home my wife grew up in. Once again, I could see that West Tennessee, with its location between Memphis and Nashville, continues to produce many historic characters both past and present.

Norbert grew up in a small town near Muscle Shoals, Alabama. Tucked in the hill and lake country in the northwest corner of Alabama, it is about a three-hour ride from Nashville. He describes Muscle Shoals as so small that "if you stole a car, they would know who did it."

His father had once played a bass fiddle in a bar on Beale Street in Memphis. His hope for Norbert was that he would go to college, get a business degree and join his father in the insurance business. Finding that course boring and unattractive, Norbert later reminisced, "From that moment on I would devote my life to the pursuit of music."

In the summer of 1956, Elvis Presley had exploded on the music scene. A whole generation was influenced by his music. Some kids from Norbert's neighborhood had decided to start a band, and since he was the only one who had access to a bass fiddle, he naturally got to play.

Despite the fact that Norbert's twelfth-grade piano teacher once said, "The boy has no talent and exhibited very poor manual dexterity," he decided to give it a try. It worked far better than he could have expected.

The band was named Glen Pettus and the Rhythm Rockets. At first, they played for local "sock hops." Moving up a step, Norbert joined a new band named Mark V, following the custom of naming your band after an expensive automobile. Four major universities were within three hours of Muscle Shoals, and the group began playing fraternity parties at Ole Miss and the University of Alabama. The band now had a new look with matching turquoise jackets. Making as much as $25 a night, Norbert thought life was pretty good for a sixteen-year-old!

After acquiring a new singer named Dan Penn, the group changed its name to Dan Penn and the Pallbearers. The name came from an old Cadillac hearse the band used to travel to wherever they played.

The Pallbearers were doing fine playing weekends, but the next step to a recording career seemed to elude them until Rick Hall opened a recording studio in an old abandoned warehouse. This was the creation of the legendary FAME Studios.

FAME stands for Florence Alabama Music Enterprises. Though there was now a recording studio, it needed a star to make it a success, and that person was Arthur Alexander, who was at the time a bellhop at the Muscle Shoals Hotel. His first song was "You Better Move On." The record made the top 10 and set Muscle Shoals as a recording center. Other artists who followed the path to Muscle Shoals were The Tams with their hit record of "What Kind of Fool Do You Think I Am?" and Jimmy Hughes with "Steal Away."

In 1965 Norbert and three others of the old Pallbearers moved to Nashville. Some of the artists Norbert played with were Chet

Atkins, Dolly and Stella Parton, Ray Charles, Linda Ronstadt, Al Hirt and Henry Mancini. Others include Kris Kristofferson, Dan Fogelberg, The Pointer Sisters and Ray Stevens.

From 1970 to 1977, Putnam played bass in 120 songs with Elvis Presley. He is even mentioned in one Elvis recording of "Merry Christmas, Baby" when Elvis calls, "Wake up, Put!"

In 1970, Norbert changed roles from being a part of the band to producer. The move occurred when Kristofferson asked Norbert to take his place and produce an album by Joan Baez, five minutes before they were to begin. The recording was an instant success with the song "The Night They Drove Ole Dixie Down," which went all the way to number three on the Billboard Top 100 chart.

Outside of the years Norbert played with Elvis, he is best known for his production of Jimmy Buffett, who had such songs as "Margaritaville," "Cheeseburger in Paradise" and "Changes in Latitude" among the albums they produced. Other artists he produced included Dave Loggins, Fogelberg and Kristofferson.

Norbert lived in Jackson for a little over two years. Just as we were really beginning to fully understand his greatness, he was gone. In 2015, he returned to Muscle Shoals, the place where it all began.

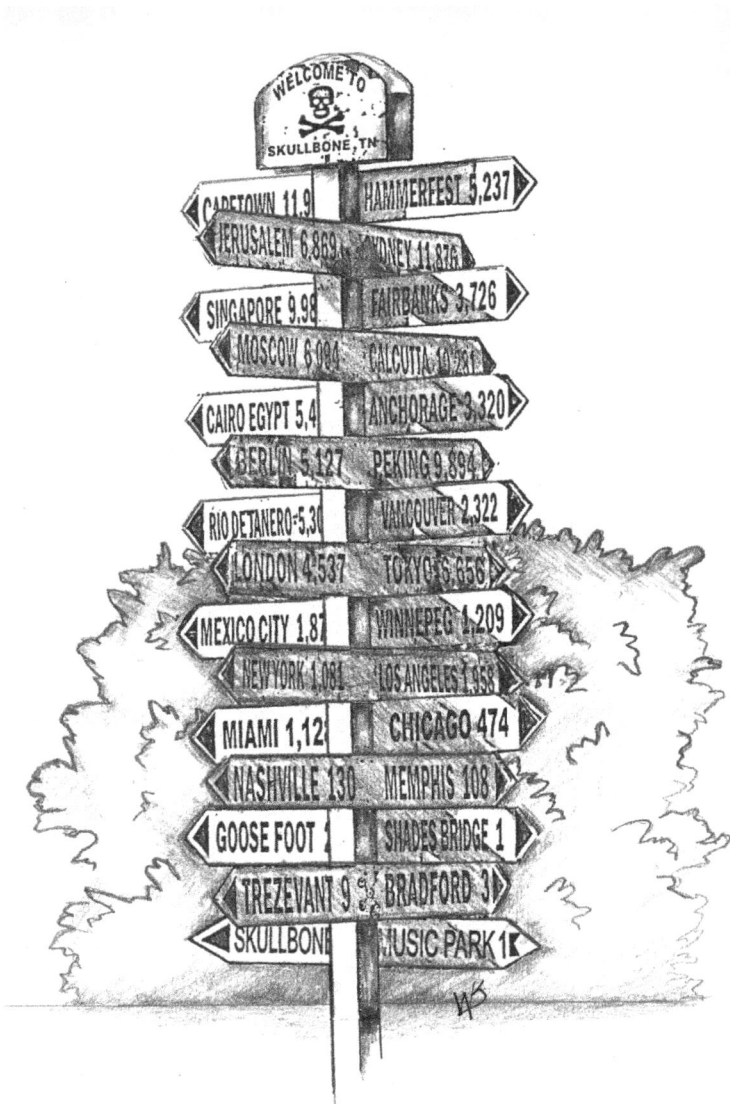

Skullbone was famous for many things including this sign and bare-knuckle boxing.

Chapter 21

Skullbone

West Tennessee certainly has its share of towns with colorful names. For example, there is Sweet Lips in Chester County. The name comes from early settlers who said that the water from a nearby spring was "sweet to their lips."

An even more colorful name is Frog Jump, located in Crockett County. But that hasn't always been the name. It was once named Davis Springs, but an early settler changed the name to Lightning Bug and Frog Jump because of the numbers of bugs and frogs. Other names abound such as Gold Dust, Tiger Tail, Edith, Graball, Finger and Nankipoo.

My favorite town with an unusual name is Skullbone, located near Bradford in northeastern Gibson County. "North Gibson," as it was called in the earliest days of the county, was a river

Facebook video library
https://goo.gl/nKdgqC

port on the South Fork of the Obion River. Boat traffic on the Obion declined after 1873 when the I.C. Railroad was built, and shipping and commercial traffic moved to Bradford.

There are many stories about how the name Skullbone came about. One early writer, obviously confused, referred to the little village as "Skin Bone." Some historians claim that a man named Allen Maxey, for the amusement of bystanders, would allow himself to be struck in the head for a drink of whiskey. Regardless of its origin, the name of the community is Skullbone. Even more important, it is more than a town; it is part of a kingdom — Skullbonia. And the people who live there are called Skullbonians.

The type of fighting was first called "fist and skull bone." The boxers could only hit each other on the head or skull bone, hence the name Skullbone. To hit below the collar was a foul. Only knockdowns counted as rounds. Time had nothing to do with the fight. The fight was not over until one man or his seconds said "enough." Fights were scheduled on a regular basis, somewhat like boxing matches today. By the time the railroads came, "fist and skull" fighting began to die out. Do you think these early fighters were tougher than the boxers of today? You be the judge. However, one measure of their toughness can be found in the way they played baseball. They did not use gloves! Can you imagine catching a ninety-miles-per-hour fastball without a glove?

Skullbone can be described as a peninsula mostly of Republicans, jutting down from Weakley and Carroll counties into a sea of Democrats in Gibson County. The Civil War was a difficult time for maintaining law and order. A company of the 7th Cavalry, U.S., was composed of soldiers from Skullbone.

Other soldiers joined the Confederacy. Postwar family reunions show Union and Confederate soldiers from the same family.

Today, Hampton's General Store is the only store in Skullbone. For all practical purposes, Hampton's Store is Skullbone. It sits at the junction of Skullbone Road and State Route 105. The front of the building has a sign that tells the whole story: "Skullbone: Kingdom of Skullbonia at Hampton's Store. City Hall and Mayor's Office upstairs." The community has never been incorporated and there is no real mayor. The post office closed in 1903.

Near the store is a sign that gives the mileage to thirty different locations from Skullbone. While the communities of Goose Foot and Shade's Bridge are less than a mile away, Sydney, Australia, is 11,879 miles away! Skullbone is one of the most unique villages in West Tennessee. Have a sandwich in Hampton's Store and relive the days of "bare-knuckle" fights.

In 1953, Governor Gordon Browning issued this proclamation: "Whereas, since my earliest childhood I have known of a mystic realm not far away known as Skullbone some of whose fluid borders were indefinite, but whose name seemed to originate from the practice of fist and skull combat between men in the early days which was more for entertainment than for vengeance ... Now, therefore, I, Gordon Browning, Governor of Tennessee, in order to dispel any doubts about the wholesomeness and justified pride of a great region do hereby recognize and proclaim the existence of the Territory of Skullbonia down in West Tennessee — as a place of tradition and song and happiness as a delightful place to live and a worthy successor to the rugged frontiersmen who built its early traditions."

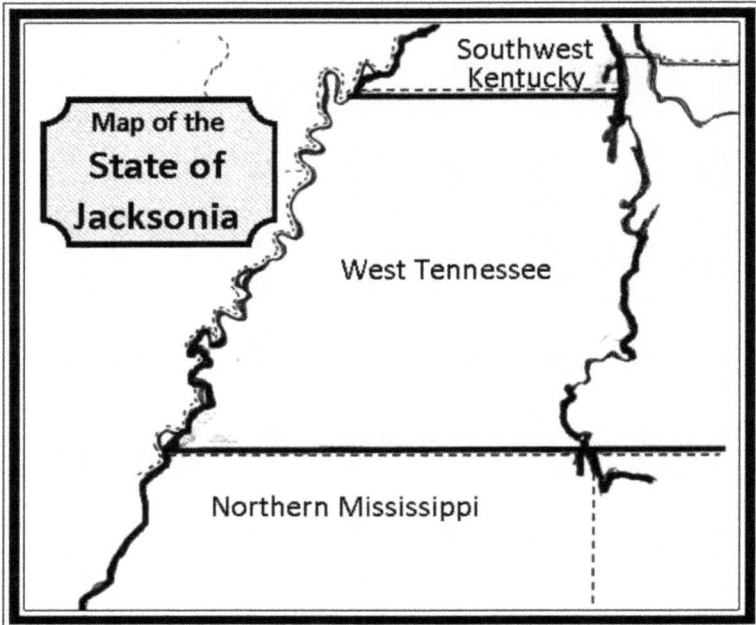

In 1841, Andrew Johnson introduced a bill in the Senate for the secession of East Tennessee to be called "the State of Franklin." To counterbalance this, John A. Gardner introduced a resolution for the creation of a new "State of Jacksonia" out of the former territory of the Chickasaws.

Chapter 22

The State of Jacksonia

A custom of Native American tribes was to tell the stories of the tribe's history to the young people. In this way, their history could be kept alive for future generations. As a historian and a writer, I sometimes feel like one of those storytellers of long ago.

An old story recently brought to life is about sectionalism in Tennessee and how West Tennessee could have been affected.

Because of the unusual shape of the state of Tennessee, it is only normal that sectionalism has been suggested or promoted through the years. In 1802 a French traveler said that "East and West Tennessee would eventually form two states."

In 1841, Andrew Johnson introduced a bill in the Senate for the secession of East Tennessee to be called "the State of

Facebook video library
https://goo.gl/nKdgqC

Franklin." To counterbalance this, John A. Gardner introduced a resolution for the creation of a new "State of Jacksonia" out of the former territory of the Chickasaws.

The Huntingdon Advertiser supported this idea for the creation of a new state made up of western Tennessee, northern Mississippi and the portion of Kentucky that lies west of the Tennessee River. The movement to establish "Jacksonia" was defeated in the Senate by a vote of 9-14. If it had passed, Jackson or Memphis would have been the capital.

Thirty-two years later, the idea of West Tennessee "breaking away" and forming a separate state came up again. West Tennessee newspapers tell the story, despite the fact that Jackson newspapers of the period no longer exist.

The July 25, 1873, edition of the Bolivar Bulletin reported the following: "The proposed new state to be formed from North Mississippi, all of Western Tennessee and Southwestern Kentucky caused a convention to be held in Bolivar to select delegates to a Jackson convention to be held July 29, 1873." A list of the proposed delegates then followed with 107 names of the delegates.

Six days later, the Somerville Falcon reported: "West Tennessee has been constantly ignored in the distribution of state honors by Middle and East Tennessee and has only been useful to those superior sections when enormous revenues were to be raised or when they had some favorite candidate for high office who was looking for votes. We are divided from these sections by natural boundaries and by a difference of climate. We have no common interests and ought to be separated. Sooner or later this will be effected!"

The last reference to the proposed new state is from the Bolivar paper one week later on August 8: "We have been assured by gentlemen of influence that outside the press of Memphis, the people of Memphis favor a new state."

These articles in the Bolivar and Somerville papers are the only reference to the forming of a new state in West Tennessee. Something had to happen, but what was it? If Hardeman County elected 107 delegates, and every county in West Tennessee, North Mississippi and Southwestern Kentucky did a similar thing, there would have been thousands of delegates!

It never happened because Tennessee is still one state. Today, the internet, interstate highways and modern technology bring us closer together.

And yet, I would love to find out the rest of the story, and what became of the idea of a new state with its capital in West Tennessee. Perhaps someday we will find out.

Entertainer Tina Turner put herself and her hometown of Nutbush on the map when she became famous.

Chapter 23

Tina Turner, International Entertainer

The little community of Nutbush, Tennessee, in rural Haywood County hasn't changed much since settlers from North Carolina and Kentucky came there in the early nineteenth century. Never large, over the last seventy-five years Nutbush has grown even smaller. Most of the sharecropper families are gone, replaced by modern farming equipment. Though Nutbush is still recognized for its cotton production, it is best known as the childhood home of Tina Turner.

Tina was born Anna Mae Bullock in 1939. One of two children, she had an older sister named Aillene. The family lived on the Poindexter Farm, where her father was a sharecropper. When World War II came along, her parents and older sister moved to Knoxville to work in a defense plant. Anna Mae

Facebook video library
https://goo.gl/nKdgqC

was left in Nutbush to live with her grandparents. After the war, the family returned to Nutbush to live in the Flagg Grove community where Anna Mae attended Flagg Grove Community School from the first through the eighth grade.

When she was eleven, her mother left and moved to St. Louis. Two years later, her father remarried and moved to Detroit. Abandoned for a second time, Anna Mae and her sister were sent to live with another grandmother in Brownsville, where Anna Mae attended Carver High School. When her grandmother died three years later, she went to live with her mother in St. Louis. After graduating from high school, she went to work at Barnes-Jewish Hospital with dreams of becoming a nurse.

When she was eighteen, Anna Mae and her sister began to frequent night clubs in St. Louis and East St. Louis. One night in East St. Louis, she saw Ike Turner and his band, The Kings of Rhythm, and said Ike's music "put her in a trance." At a later show, she was given a chance to sing during intermission. Upon hearing her voice, Ike allowed her to be a guest vocalist with the band.

In 1960, Ike wrote a rhythm and blues song titled "A Fool in Love." When Art Lassister, the main singer for the band, failed to show up for a recording session, Anna Mae stepped in, and a star was instantly created. When Henry "Juggy" Murray, the president of the R&B label Sue Records, heard the tape, he said her vocals "sounded like screaming dirt ... it was a funky sound." Murray convinced Ike to make Anna Mae the star of the show.

It was at this point Ike Turner changed Anna Mae's name to Tina because the name rhymed with the television character

Sheena. Anna Mae was gone and forgotten. From now on, her name was Tina Turner.

As the Ike and Tina Turner Revue toured the country, their popularity grew. One writer cited them as "one of the most hottest, most durable and potentially most explosive of all R&B ensembles." Maintaining their momentum through a rigorous schedule, the duo performed ninety straight nights in shows across the country. In 1969, they toured as the opening act for the Rolling Stones, winning even more fans.

In 1973, the duo had a top five hit in the United Kingdom titled "Nutbush City Limits," an autobiographical song of Tina's childhood.

Despite their musical success, the couple frequently had marital problems. Ike was often physically abusive. In 1978, the couple divorced with Tina citing Ike's frequent infidelities, physical abuse and his increasing drug and alcohol dependency.

When Tina left Ike, she had thirty-six cents and a gas credit card. To make ends meet and to care for her children, she used food stamps and cleaned houses.

By 1983, Tina's career began to gain momentum with new recordings and videos. In 1984, her solo album *Private Dancer* was released. It won four Grammy Awards and sold more than twenty million copies worldwide. One of the singles on the album, "What's Love Got to Do With It," reached No. 1 on U.S. pop charts and earned the Grammy for Record of the Year. Though she was in her mid-forties, she was becoming even more renowned for her uniquely energetic performances with her short skirts, signature legs and punk hairstyle.

In 1989, she returned to the screen and played opposite Mel Gibson in the film *Mad Max Beyond Thunderdome*. The next year she released her second solo album. In the following decade, another album was released. She also did several recordings for film soundtracks including the James Bond title song, "Goldeneye," and "He Lives in You" for *The Lion King*.

In 1991, Ike and Tina Turner were inducted into the Rock and Roll Hall of Fame. Ike was unable to attend the ceremony as he was serving a prison sentence for drug possession. He died of a drug overdose in 2007.

When Tina embarked on her "Tina! 50th Anniversary Tour," she announced it would be her final tour. Following the end of the tour, she essentially retired from the music industry except for occasional appearances and recordings. In 2013, at age 73, she married longtime partner and German record executive Erwin Bach, just months after gaining her Swiss citizenship.

It has been quite a journey for Anna Mae Bullock, now Tina Turner. The girl with the million-dollar legs has come from the cotton fields of Haywood County to the lakes of Switzerland. She no longer comes back. The days of coming home are a thing of the past. And yet West Tennessee still remembers her.

"Miss Ollie," Jackson's famous madam, ran her business from this modest home. During World War II, the commander of the 101st Airborne at Fort Campbell, Kentucky, threatened to shut Miss Ollie down because he had too many AWOL soldiers.

Chapter 24

Jackson's Madam

This is a hard story to write because of its sensitive nature. For years people have asked me why I never wrote about Ollie Pope. I have always avoided the subject, however "Miss Ollie" was part of the history of Jackson and West Tennessee. So perhaps it is time to write what I know about one of our more colorful and controversial characters.

Martha Blue Bell Hemby was born in January 1887 in Henderson County, and lived in Jackson and Madison County most of her life. In the 1910 Census, Ollie Hemby, 23, single, is listed along with her illegitimate daughter in the Dyer County Poor House. There is no mention to be found of her daughter Beatrice again.

The following year a farm laborer named Hammie Pope of

Gibson County proposed to and married Ollie. By the following year, Ollie and Hammie lived in Jackson at 168 South Street.

In 1912 Ollie was charged by the Madison County Grand Jury with keeping a house of "ill fame." Found guilty, she was fined two dollars. Apparently she did not learn her lesson from the experience and returned to the same courtroom in 1913 and again in 1915. On the third time, the court was tougher and fined her twenty dollars and sent her to the Madison County Jail and Workhouse. After thirty days, she could only be released when she paid the twenty-dollar fine. Unable to pay the fine, Ollie spent six months in jail before being declared insolvent and released.

In 1919 Ollie bought the house at 522 South Liberty Street for five hundred and fifty dollars. This house would become her home and place of business for the next thirty-five years. There was nothing unusual about the house. White frame with a front porch, it was just like other houses in the neighborhood — except it wasn't!

Ollie Pope was a small woman. Kent Gardner, in a newspaper article, described her as being small and dignified with a gimpy leg. Other Jacksonians remember her as a small woman with a bad leg. She had medium brown hair, walked with a cane and in later years wore glasses. Apparently, Ollie had polio as a young girl, which caused her to use a cane throughout her life.

She was a good businesswoman in the bad times of the Great Depression and World War II. The nature of her business was what made it unusual. Ollie Pope was a madam, and her employees were prostitutes.

Prostitution was illegal in those years as it is today. Most people knew about her business. And yet, she somehow stayed in business for more than three decades. There is no written history of Miss Ollie. To understand her and what she did is best obtained through oral history to hear the stories of Miss Ollie and "her girls."

In the years she operated her business, downtown Jackson was the center of everything. The move north had not begun. Many of the larger churches were downtown, including Catholics, Baptists, Methodists, Presbyterians and Episcopalians. City hall, the police and sheriff were within a five-minute walk. And yet her business continued to operate successfully as usual. How could that happen?

Miss Ollie kept good control of her employees and their customers. Drunks and troublemakers were not welcome. If the police were selling tickets for some charity events, Miss Ollie was their best customer. Every week a prominent Jackson physician came to the house for a medical exam of all the girls.

In those years there were only three banks, all located within a block of each other. Banking hours were from 9 a.m. to 2 p.m. Monday through Friday. On Mondays, fifteen minutes after the bank closed, a bank employee would open a side door, and the girls would come in to do their banking. On Monday they went to First National Bank, Tuesday to the Second National Bank and on Wednesday they went to the National Bank of Commerce.

A popular story at Second National Bank was about a very large, gruff vice president who never stood up when customers came in. The one exception was when Miss Ollie brought one

355

of the girls into the bank — a very attractive redhead — and the vice president stood up!

Miss Ollie stories are still told today even though those who were involved have been dead for years. One story was about a teenager who cut Miss Ollie's grass in hopes of being allowed to visit with the girls. When his father's car pulled up, the teenager hid under the front steps while his parent went inside.

During World War II, the commander of the 101st Airborne at Fort Campbell, Kentucky, threatened to come to Jackson to shut the business down because so many of his soldiers went AWOL in Jackson.

One employee, Margo Jobson, was the source of many stories. Redheaded and beautiful, she is still talked about today. Her life came to a tragic end when a deputy sheriff shot and killed her following an argument in the parking lot of the Green Lantern, a bar east of Jackson, and then killed himself.

Perhaps Miss Ollie is best remembered for what happened when she died in May 1954. Smith Funeral Home was in charge of the funeral. Two of its young employees began calling prominent citizens and elected officials, telling them they had been selected as pallbearers. There was an immediate flight out of Jackson! Her nephews served as pallbearers, and she was buried in Hollywood Cemetery.

Miss Ollie was one of Jackson's most unusual business people. Few people are still alive who knew her, and yet there has been a bar named for her in downtown Jackson. Go there for a drink someday and see if anyone remembers Jackson's madam.

History tells us that Miss Ollie was born in January 1887 in

Henderson County. She died in May 1954 and is buried next to her sister in Hollywood Cemetery. Her home at 522 South Liberty Street has long since been torn down.

One mystery still exists. Many accounts of Miss Ollie describe her carrying a small black book, presumably with names and phone numbers in it of her customers. I wonder what happened to it? Perhaps it is best the little black book has never been found.

Brigadier General Frank C. Armstrong directed his troops during "The Armstrong Raid," which included battles at Britton Lane, Bolivar and Medon Station.

Chapter 25

The Armstrong Raid Including the Battles of Bolivar, Medon Station & Britton Lane

It was late summer of the second year of the war, and throughout the South expectant eyes would soon watch two Confederate armies as they invaded Northern territory. One was under Robert E. Lee and was moving toward Maryland, and the other was under Braxton Bragg and was moving toward Kentucky. For the Confederacy, this was a time of hope. In April, the Confederacy had been on the defensive. New Orleans had been lost, General George McClellan was in front of Richmond and Major General Henry Halleck was about to take Corinth. But by August, the Southern nation was on the offensive.

In the west, Bragg's objective was to drive Major General Don Carlos Buell out of Kentucky and Tennessee. In order to move

Facebook video library
https://goo.gl/nKdgqC

against Buell, however, someone would have to keep General Ulysses S. Grant occupied in western Tennessee and northern Mississippi so that he could not send reinforcements to Buell. This job fell to Major General Sterling Price, who was in command of the Army of the West at Tupelo, Mississippi. To contain Grant and keep him from reinforcing Buell, Price planned to attack Major General William Rosecrans at Corinth, Mississippi, and to send cavalry raids to cut Grant's communications along the Mississippi Central R.R. in western Tennessee.

Before Price could use his cavalry, he had to reorganize them. The cavalry had been dismounted in Arkansas before Price assumed control, and as a result, his mounted forces numbered less than a thousand. To facilitate their reorganization, Frank C. Armstrong was promoted to brigadier general in charge of the cavalry. The new general had an unusual military background. He had served with the Union forces at the first battle of Manassas, but afterward had changed over to the Southern side. Prior to taking over as head of the cavalry, he had been elected colonel of the 3rd Louisiana Infantry.

With the departure of General William J. Hardee for Chattanooga on July 29, Price began making plans to attack the Federal stronghold at Corinth; however, because of difficulties in uniting with General Earl Van Dorn's troops, the attack had to be rescheduled again and again. It was not until August 24 that Van Dorn announced that he was ready to cooperate with Price, and even then it would take him two more weeks to move his troops. Price, realizing that something must be done to divert Grant's attention, decided to send his newly organized cavalry into western Tennessee to destroy supplies and communications.

Thus, because of the inability of the Confederate chieftains to cooperate with each other, the newly organized cavalry under Colonel Frank Armstrong was ordered into action.

Armstrong's command left Guntown, Mississippi, at daybreak on Friday, August 22. For many of the raw troops, this was their first chance for action. Others in the various units had seen action at Shiloh and around Corinth, but for all of them, it would be their first chance to act together as the cavalry of the Army of the West. When Armstrong left, he had four regiments plus one battalion of cavalry. These troops were Barteau's Second Tennessee Cavalry, the Second Arkansas Cavalry under Colonel W.F. Slemons, Wirt Adams' cavalry, Wheeler's Cavalry and Balch's Battalion.

In all, they numbered about eleven hundred men. They were in good condition, and as one of the soldiers put it: "Generally speaking, they were a well-mounted and fine-looking bunch of men."

Armstrong moved his men along rapidly. Traveling southwest and then northwest, they covered forty-three miles in the first three days. The night of August 24 found them camped on the bank of Cypress Creek. On the 25th, they marched sixteen miles to the Tippah River, where they encamped, and on the following morning, the leading regiment entered Holly Springs, Mississippi, as the town clock struck nine. After remaining in town for about ten minutes, they continued on to the north for five miles where they stopped and bivouacked on the banks of the Coldwater River.

While in the vicinity of Holly Springs, they were strengthened by three more cavalry regiments under the command of Colonel William H. Jackson. These troops were the First Mississippi Cavalry under Colonel R.A. Pinson; the Second Missouri Cavalry under Colonel Robert McCulloch; and the Seventh Tennessee Cavalry under Colonel William H. Jackson. Jackson had been informed of the purpose of the raid and, prior to Armstrong's arrival, had sent two spies to Jackson, Tennessee, to obtain information concerning the fortifications there. These two men — William Witherspoon of Jackson and Allen Shaw of Carroll County, Tennessee, both members of the Seventh Tennessee Cavalry — had been captured by a roving patrol of the Second Illinois Cavalry but, after having been taken to Jackson, had managed to talk the Federal authorities into freeing them. Soon after this they made their way back to Holly Springs and joined their comrades.

The combined troops, now numbering around 3,500, rested in their camps until about 3 p.m. on the following afternoon. After breaking camp, they traveled close to sixteen miles, not stopping until late that night when they made their camp on a branch of the Wolf River, within four miles of LaGrange, Tennessee. Here the horses and men rested on the 28th. Armstrong realized that there would be little rest once contact had been made with the enemy forces.

Meanwhile, telegraph wires within the Federal lines were buzzing with news of Armstrong's advance. On the 28th, while the Confederates rested on the Wolf River, Grant received a message from General Henry W. Halleck asking for further reinforcements for Buell. In reply to this, Grant cautioned that he would not be able to spare very many troops as he was about to be attacked by large numbers of Confederate cavalry. On the same day, Grant sent a message to one of his subordinates saying, "It is reported that a rebel force of 6,000 cavalry have been sent to attack our lines. Keep a sharp look out."

On the following day, Colonel Elias Dennis, commander of two Illinois regiments at Estenaula, Tennessee, wrote to Colonel M.K. Lawler that Bragg was at Guntown with an army of seven brigades and 6,000 cavalry. He further wrote that Bragg had advanced 2,000 cavalry to within five miles of LaGrange. Also that day, General G.M. Dodge at Trenton, Tennessee, sent the following dispatch to Captain M. Rochester at Columbus, Kentucky:

"From all the information I can obtain there is some movement in contemplation in West Tennessee by the rebels. They are massing all their cavalry; have drawn in all their guerilla bands, and everything is very quiet. General Grant telegraphed me last night that they had massed 6,000 cavalry and intended to attack our lines at some point."

Thus Grant was surprisingly well-informed on just where Armstrong was even though General Grant had grossly overestimated Armstrong's strength.

In the saddle once again on Friday the 29th, the Confederates crossed the Memphis and Charleston Railroad at LaGrange, Tennessee. Leaving there around noon, they continued on to within nine miles of Bolivar where they spent the night. For some unexplained reason, the Federals in Bolivar were unaware of the danger that they were in, even though the rest of the surrounding outposts had been alerted. Late in the day on the 29th, Colonel Marcellus M. Crocker, commander of the post, had received a report that there was an enemy force of about 400 men threatening him on the Guntown Road. Obviously enough he was in for a big surprise.

Early next morning, two companies of the 20th Ohio under Major John C. Fry found themselves groping toward the Confederates. Their task was to guard their lines and to feel out the enemy's position. A short time later, Colonel Mortimer D. Leggett, commander of the First Brigade, sent out forty-five mounted infantry from the 78th Ohio to support Major Fry and his two companies. These mounted infantry, or "mule cavalry" as they were called, were in turn followed by Colonel Leggett himself with the balance of the 20th Ohio and three additional companies of the 78th Ohio.

Leaving his forces at a picket post on the Grand Junction Road, Colonel Leggett and his staff rode on to some woods on the Van Buren Road. Leggett's forces were instructed to await the arrival of two pieces of artillery of the Ninth Indiana Battery. Colonel Leggett soon found Major Fry with his two companies of the 20th Ohio along with the "mule cavalry" from the 78th Ohio engaged in a heavy skirmish. One look was enough to convince Leggett that he had greatly underestimated the Confederate strength. He immediately sent back for the forces at the picket post on the Grand Junction Road to come forward as quickly as possible. A few moments later, Leggett gained a position where he could see all of the Confederate forces and realized how greatly he was outnumbered. In his report of the affair, he wrote, "I gained a position where I had a distinct view of the foe and found that I was contending with a force of over 6,000 instead of 300 or 400."

The Federals had been caught in a trap set by their own failure to maintain proper communication with other posts. Their forces at the time numbered less than 200. It would be another two hours before they would be reinforced. Retreat was impossible as indicated by another excerpt from Leggett's report:

"At this time I would have withdrawn my little force from the contest, having less than one man to twenty of the enemy, but the nature of the ground over which I would have been obliged to retreat was such, that my force must have been annihilated had I attempted to escape from such overwhelming numbers. I had not enough men to retreat, and consequently had no choice left but to fight until support could reach us."

What Leggett had taken to be 6,000 men was nothing more than two of Armstrong's cavalry regiments. These two regiments were the 2nd Missouri Cavalry under Colonel Robert McCulloch and the 2nd Arkansas Cavalry under Colonel W.F. Slemons. The rest of the Confederate cavalry did not leave their camps until noon. In all probability, Armstrong was waiting for his scouts to report to him, but his delay in bringing up additional troops permitted the Yankees to avoid destruction. Within a short time, two companies of the 11th Illinois Cavalry under Major S.D. Putterbaugh arrived and were thrown into the fray. For the next two hours, the fight continued as nothing more than a long-range skirmish. This gift of time saved the Federals because it gave them the chance they needed to bring up reinforcements. Had the Confederates charged the Yankee position at any time during this two-hour interval, it would have been a simple matter to capture them. Now it was too late.

Federal reinforcements arrived in the form of six companies of the 20th Ohio under Colonel Manning Force plus two pieces of artillery under Lieutenant Wallace Hight of the 9th Indiana Battery. So precarious was the position of the Federals at this time that the battery was sent back again to the junction of the Van Buren and Middleburg roads to ensure its safety.

Around noon the Confederates began sweeping around the right flank in an all-out effort to break through and encircle the Federals. Leggett and his men were in a desperate situation again, but reinforcements from Bolivar arrived just in time. These consisted of two companies of the 78th Ohio and two companies of the 20th Ohio, all under the command of a captain named Chandler, and the 2nd Illinois Cavalry under the command of Colonel Harvey Hogg. The reinforcements were placed to the right and left of the Middleburg Road to bridge the gap between Leggett's forces and those of Colonel Force that were arriving from the Van Buren Road, where they had been engaged.

The Confederates charged down the Middleburg Road three times, each time being firmly repulsed. Then with a bound to the right, the two Confederate regiments under McCulloch and Slemons bore down on Colonel Harvey Hogg and his Illinois cavalrymen. Badly outnumbered, Hogg gave the command, "Forward, give them cold steel, boys," and met the Confederates with a countercharge. In the next instant the two lines came together and merged into a large mass of horses and men, each force trying to destroy the other. Colonel Hogg, at the head of his cavalry, sought out the lead Confederate commander, Colonel McCulloch of the 2nd Missouri Cavalry. Just as Hogg was about to attack McCulloch, he was torn from his saddle by a volley of Confederate rifle fire. Later examination of Hogg's body showed that he had been hit nine times! The Federal cavalry, seeing their leader fall, wavered and fell back in confusion.

At about the same time that Hogg was killed, the Federal infantry under Colonel Leggett had been attacked, and hand-to-hand fighting had developed. The Confederates were too strong, however, and the infantry began falling back toward Bolivar. After about a mile, the Federal forces regained the use of their artillery, which had been sent to the rear, and managed to hold the Confederates off with it until they could regain the safety of their trenches in Bolivar.

The fight had lasted throughout most of the day, progressing from a skirmish in the morning on the Van Buren Road to the bitterly contested fighting in the afternoon on the Middleburg Road. The Federals, under colonels Leggett and Force, had done a creditable job in holding off superior forces all day without being captured.

The Confederates under McCulloch and Slemons had won a tactical victory in driving the Federals back into Bolivar, but it was an empty victory in that the Federals had escaped capture. Had the remainder of the Confederate cavalry been used, there would have been little chance for the Federals. There is little excuse for Armstrong's failure to employ all of his units.

The Federals reported their losses in the affair to be eighteen wounded, five killed and sixty-four captured. The Federal estimate of the Confederate losses ran as high as 200, but this is only a guess as the Confederates did not indicate their losses. The only Confederate officer to be killed was Captain John Rock Champion of the 2nd Missouri Cavalry, who was killed at about the same time as Colonel Hogg.

This was the first time that many of the Confederates had been under fire. Edwin H. Fay, a Louisiana soldier, remarked:

"The Yanks fired on us with a Battery of Artillery and threw shell all around but did no damage, then ran back into Bolivar. We had five men wounded, two shot themselves after the battle, accidentally."

John Milton Hubbard of Company E, 7th Tennessee Cavalry, observed:

"Captain Champion of the 2nd Missouri was killed here. As his body was borne from the field by two of his troopers, I saw for the first time a dead Confederate who had been slain in battle."

The Confederates left the battlefield a little before sunset, going around to the west of Bolivar, where they bivouacked for the night within three miles of Whiteville on Clearwater Creek.

While the Confederates rested for a few hours, Yankee officials were hurriedly sending dispatches and rearranging forces. Armstrong had thrown a scare into top Union commanders, even though they were informed of his arrival. Now the Federals were faced with the problem of stopping Armstrong and his raiders before they could reach Jackson, Tennessee, which was described by Brigadier General Leonard R. Ross as being "Weakly [sic] garrisoned and without fortifications."

On the same day of the Confederate attack at Bolivar, the commander of the post at Jackson, Tennessee, M.K. Lawler, sent the following dispatch to the commander of the post at Bethel, Tennessee, Colonel I.N. Haynie:

"You will hold your command in readiness to resist any demonstration of the enemy. Brisk skirmishing is now going on at Bolivar. That place attacked by about 4,000 cavalry."

To protect Jackson, the Federal force at Estenaula, Tennessee, under Colonel Dennis, was ordered to report to Jackson at once. This force consisted of the 20th Illinois Infantry under Captain Orton Frisbee; the 30th Illinois under Major Warren Shedd; Gumbart's Artillery, which was Battery E of the Second Illinois artillery; and two companies of cavalry under Captain John S. Foster, designated as the 4th Ohio Cavalry companies. These troops struck tents on the morning of the 31st, destroying excess stores and baggage, and began their march toward Jackson.

Meanwhile the Confederates encamped near Bolivar had eaten supper around 11 p.m. and had gone quickly to sleep. They were awakened about three hours later and began marching away from Bolivar before it was light. The command crossed the Big Hatchie River about daybreak and, continuing on, struck the Mississippi Central Railroad at Toone, Tennessee. Here a detachment of Federal troops, stationed as railroad guards, began firing on the lead Confederates. The Confederates surrounded the Federals and forced them to surrender before they could offer further resistance. Forty-two of the guards were captured and one was killed. A few Confederates were wounded.

The trestlework at Toone was burned and the telegraph wires were cut before the gray-clad horsemen galloped off down the railroad toward Medon. While they were marching from Toone to Medon, a train was stopped and nearly captured. The only Confederate report to mention this is found in a letter by Edwin H. Fay to his wife.

"Heard a train coming ambushed it and if the goose in command had only torn up the track behind would have burned it but he only fire on it as it stopped to land reinforcements and a great many jumped back and the train ran back."

About 3 p.m., as the column neared Medon, Federal pickets opened fire. The lead regiment, which was the 2nd Tennessee under Colonel C.R. Barteau, dismounted several of its members, who carried long-range rifles and opened fire. After a few shots, the Federal pickets retreated behind breastworks within the town.

The breastworks consisted of bales of cotton piled up near the railroad depot. Some of the detachments, which had been stationed in front of Medon along the railroad, had preceded the Confederates into Medon and warned the Federals of the approaching danger. Consequently the breastworks of cotton had just been completed. Now about 150 men of the 45th Illinois crouched behind them awaiting the arrival of the Confederates.

Meanwhile, Colonel Michael K. Lawler, commander of the post at Jackson, had also been informed of the Rebels' presence at Medon. As a result, six companies of the 7th Missouri infantry under Major W.S. Oliver had been dispatched by train to

Jackson. These troops did not arrive until after the Confederates had encircled the fort.

Barteau's 2nd Tennessee Infantry swung around to the right of the town and stormed the barricades from the northeast side. In the meantime, other regiments were coming into town and storming the breastworks from the front. The attackers were met with a steady fire from within the barricade, and the Confederates soon found that the Yankees could not be budged without the use of artillery, and Armstrong had none at his disposal. The infantry continued firing on the barricades until about sundown when the train carrying the six companies of the 7th Missouri arrived. These troops disembarked and immediately charged, driving the Confederates before them. Darkness terminated further fighting, and the Federals soon retired within their breastworks around the depot. The Confederates drew off to the east where they settled their forces down for the night on the Casey Savage farm, just outside of Medon.

Losses for the engagement had been slight. The Yankees had had four killed and nine wounded. The Confederates had lost about twice that number. The attack had accomplished nothing. It would have been too bloody to have attacked the breastworks without artillery, and Armstrong wisely enough decided not to try the attack.

As the Confederates rested, other Federal troops were marching toward Medon to relieve the beleaguered garrison. These troops were the Federals who had been stationed at Estenaula under the command of Colonel Elias S. Dennis. As has been previously stated, they had been ordered to report to Jackson to try to head off Armstrong. Colonel Lawler, commander of the post at Jackson, upon being informed of the attack on the garrison at Medon, had quickly sent orders for these troops to turn around and march back to Medon. When the messenger reached Colonel Dennis and his command, they were only about twelve miles out of Jackson. Dennis, however, turned his troops around and marched them back toward Medon. About ten that night, they reached Denmark where they encamped.

While the Federals rested at Denmark, the Confederates at the Casey Savage farm near Medon were going to bed without either fires or supper. Men in the 7th Tennessee, who would later see service under Nathan Bedford Forrest, were beginning to make caustic remarks about the lack of food and provender. Years later, William Witherspoon of Company L, 7th Tennessee, would recall:

"My regiment, 7th Tennessee, was encamped near a cornfield, was without rations for man or beast ... at a time, 1862, when the country was full of both ... Our horses fared well and we did not grumble, like philosophers it was what would happen sometimes in a soldier's life."

Twenty-four hours later, scurrying away in retreat from the Federals at Britton Lane, the cavalry would have much harsher things to say about General Armstrong!

The Federal defenders at Medon received a pleasant surprise the next morning when the Confederates bypassed them. Passing to the west of the railroad and heading to the northwest, the Confederates were marching toward Denmark. At the same time the Federals at Denmark were moving toward Medon, little suspecting that they were now marching right into the midst of Armstrong's column of cavalry. To shorten the distance, the Federals left the main road and began marching through a narrow road known as Britton's Lane — an ordinary road fourteen feet in width with a deep gully on either side between the fence and the road.

The Federal cavalry under Captain Foster was reconnoitering several miles in advance in the vicinity of the junction of the Denmark and Medon roads, near the mouth of Britton Lane, when about ten that morning, Foster and his two companies of cavalry unexpectedly came upon the advance pickets of Armstrong's column. The Confederate pickets scurried off to inform Armstrong of the approaching troops, but for some unknown reason, it was almost noon when the pickets reached Armstrong with the news. Armstrong was eating lunch at a nearby house when he was informed that there were two regiments of infantry with supporting cavalry and artillery nearby.

Acting immediately, Armstrong led his troops forward a short distance and, upon reaching the vicinity of the mouth of Britton Lane, ordered his cavalry to dismount, throw every other lock of the fence and then mount again. Armstrong's purpose in tearing down the fences was to facilitate a charge upon Dennis and his men as they marched down the lane.

In a moment, the Confederates remounted, loaded their guns and proceeded several hundred yards toward the lane, where they again came into contact with Foster's Cavalry. The lead Confederate regiment — the 2nd Missouri, which had borne the brunt of the fighting at Bolivar — began firing away at the blue-clad horsemen and the action had begun!

The Federals, being greatly outnumbered, were forced to take a defensive position along a small ridge within a large grove of trees. They were further protected by a worm rail fence that stretched along the top of the ridge. The grove of trees was surrounded on all sides by cornfields, and Dennis selected a field in front of his infantry line to post his artillery. On the left of the artillery, within the trees, were posted companies B and G of the 20th Illinois, The remaining eight companies were posted on the right of the artillery.

Once again, as they had been in every engagement throughout the entire raid, the Federals were badly outnumbered. With seven regiments and a battalion preparing to charge them, there is little doubt that the average Yankee in that line would have preferred to have been some other place! Outside of readying themselves and their guns, there was nothing that they could do but wait. One Yankee later wrote: "In front, and on the left and right were bare fields, swarming with rebels preparing for the charge. At last, on they came, the ground fairly trembling beneath their heavy tread ..."

The Illinois troops awaited the Confederates like veterans, and veterans they were, for they had already taken part in two large battles. In the operations around Fort Donelson, the 20th Illinois had sustained losses of 132 men, including their lieutenant colonel, and a short time later the regiment had lost 136 additional men at Shiloh. Following Shiloh, the men had seen little action until they were called upon to reinforce their comrades at Medon. The Union artillery opened fire on the

Confederates and evidently surprised some of them. One of the members of a lead regiment wrote in a letter to his wife: "The Yanks were ambushed for us and the accursed Tories had led us right into it."

Large dust clouds, raised by the charging cavalry, now partially obscured the field. Other Confederate regiments were now engaged in charging against the Federal infantry in the woods. Most of the Confederates dismounted and charged on foot, but concentrated rifle fire drove them back again and again. The 30th Illinois, under Major Shedd, had come up by this time and had taken a position on the left of the Federal line.

Charging horsemen spurred their horses toward the Federal artillery a third and a fourth time, but murderous rifle fire compelled them to withdraw again. On the fifth charge against the two guns, the Confederates were at last successful in capturing and drawing the cannon off. Just which regiment took the two guns was a matter that the veterans of the various regiments disputed years later when they came together at reunions and bivouacs. Almost all of the units took part in at least one of the five charges against the artillery, so it does not really make any difference who captured them. The strongest claim is held by Company L of the 7th Tennessee Cavalry, one of the last regiments to reach the battlefield. When the regiment came into contact with the Federals, General Armstrong ordered Company L to form fours and charge the artillery, while the remainder of the regiment was ordered to dismount and charge the infantry in the woods. The twenty members of Company L apparently caught the Federal artillerymen off guard and captured them before they could reverse positions and fire on the flying horsemen. William Witherspoon of that company later wrote:

"As we got fairly started down the lane, we noticed they were ramming down the load. With a general impulse that cannon had to be reached before it could be fired. We drove in our spurs and in a mad bound were upon them. It was then and there the old much-derided double barrel as an army gun done its work perfectly. In a second of time, we twenty, not one hurt, were all that were left alive with the two brass cannon."

The artillery was then taken to the east end of the lane where one piece of it was spiked and the other was thrown into a well.

While this was going on, the other units were hurling themselves across the field right up to the fence where the Yankees were posted. The result of this was appalling, as evidence by the gray-clad figures that littered the field. Some of the Confederates succeeded in reaching the fence, only to be killed upon trying to climb over it. Company E, 7th Tennessee Cavalry, came under such a heavy fire near the fence that one member of that company, John Milton Hubbard, later wrote: "How so many men ever got out of that field alive is one of those unaccountable things that sometimes occur in war."

About 3 p.m., Armstrong decided that he had had enough and called off the remaining Confederates. Dusk on that September day found them moving slowly toward the Hatchie River. At the time they had eighty Federal prisoners with them, which slowed them considerably. Not stopping at dark, they continued on until about 3 a.m. when they stopped near the Hatchie River. Behind them they left 179 dead whom the Federals buried in common graves. Many more wounded comrades had been left in houses surrounding the battlefield to await treatment of their wounds.

Most of the Confederates were discouraged by the outcome of the battle, feeling that Armstrong had handled his forces poorly. On previous nights they had complained because of lack of food and provender. Now they were beginning to question Armstrong's ability as a commander. Years later Confederate reminiscences would contain such references as this:

"We were certainly on the run, to say the last, a forced march, not halting or stopping until we ferried across the Hatchie, six miles distant, on a ferry boat. Where does the blame lie? Certainly not with the men, they carried out every order and executed it as completely as the 7th Tennessee did."

Another wrote:

"The whole command was discouraged by the operations of this raid, and thought that, if we had gained anything at all, we had paid dearly for it."

Obviously enough, the Confederates had good reason to be unhappy. Simply by encircling the Yankee regiments, Armstrong probably could have secured their capture. Instead, he chose to send regiment after regiment across an open field to certain destruction.

One Confederate later compared Armstrong with the "Wizard of the Saddle," Nathan Bedford Forrest, and decided:

"Is it not shameful that our troops were so managed as to suffer a loss of such magnitude with no corresponding good? What if Forrest had been there instead of Armstrong. Colonel Dennis would have been crushed as easily as an eggshell, with not probably the loss of one-half a dozen men."

Instead, the Federals, being well-protected by the woods and fences, received a negligible loss of four killed and approximately sixty-five wounded.

On September 2, the Confederate command crossed the Big Hatchie River approximately ten miles below where they had crossed before. By midnight on September 3, the dusty column had retraced its way back to within five miles of LaGrange, Tennessee. After this, there were no more actions with the Federals. All that was left for them to do was to return to their Mississippi base on the Mobile and Ohio railroad. By September 7, they were in Ripley, Mississippi, after having rested for two days on the Wolf River. From Ripley they traveled on a direct northern route back to their base. By the 8th, they were within twelve miles of Baldwin, Mississippi. On September 9, the weary Confederates came into Baldwin and the raid was at an end.

Tactically speaking, they had accomplished their mission in that they had diverted Grant from sending further reinforcements to Don Carlos Buell. Militarily speaking, however, Armstrong had allowed himself to be outmaneuvered by much smaller forces. In all of the actions that he had commanded, he had evidenced a basic lack of knowledge of tactics. But brighter days were ahead for Armstrong. In later years of the war, he would become a trusted leader under Forrest.

For the cavalry of the Army of the West, there was little chance to rest. On the day after they returned to Baldwin, they were called upon to take part in the campaign of Sterling Price, which resulted in the Battle of Iuka, Mississippi. In this campaign the cavalry performed in an efficient manner, and it became obvious that their campaign into western Tennessee had given them experience, if nothing else.

Today, almost 160 years since General Armstrong and his butternut cavalry came sweeping down through West Tennessee, there are few traces of the raid. At the site of the Battle of Britton Lane, near Denmark, Tennessee, is an obscure stone marker that stands about fifty feet away from the roadside. The inscription on this marker reads:

"Erected by John Ingram Bivouac, September 1, 1897, to honor an unknown number of Confederate soldiers who fell in battle on this field, September 1, 1862, and many of whom are buried here."

In 1897 neighborhood residents searched the battlefield and gathered up all the relics that they could find. The relics included buttons, gun parts, brass rings and bits of bone. The graves of the Confederate soldiers were also excavated and the remains found in these graves, along with other relics, were buried just behind and to the right of the stone monument on the battlefield. Today there is a small mound that marks the site of these relics.

For years, members of the John Ingram Bivouac would gather on the old battlefield to tell their stories of the battle. Now all of these soldiers are dead, and the monument stands, almost forgotten, as a symbol of the bravery of the men who died there so long ago.

David Crockett, politician and pioneer, cut a trail all the way to his death at The Alamo. It was Crockett who introduced a bill in the state legislature to create Gibson County.

Chapter 26

Old Times in Trenton: Crockett and Forrest

Some towns catch history like a spider catches bugs. Some have a lot of history; some have none. Even worse are towns that have historic people and events, but never recognize them. Trenton, Tennessee, has historic events and people, and it knows it!

Trenton is the county seat of Gibson County. The courthouse sits in the middle of the town. The present building is the fifth courthouse to be constructed. The previous building lasted for sixty years. Still, the county court resisted spending the money to build a new one.

In 1897 a Methodist Conference was held in Trenton with preachers and laymen from all over West Tennessee. One of the laymen, Colonel A.W. Stovall from Jackson, wrote a poem that

Facebook video library
https://goo.gl/nKdgqC

was published in the Trenton and Jackson newspapers. It read:

"I spent the day in Trenton on annual conference day,
And delegates were plentiful, both clerical and lay,
The people they are cheerful and meet you with a smile,
But Trenton needs a courthouse more up to date in style.

She's seven miles of sidewalk well-laid with brick and sand,
And nicer streets and houses are nowhere in the land,
She has three learned judges and lawyers all the while,
But Trenton's old-time courthouse is out of date and style."

The Methodists won the battle. A new courthouse was started two years later. The building was completed in July 1901, twenty-seven months after it started. One problem arose after the building was completed when the janitor resigned because of the size of the building and the three hundred brass spittoons that needed to be cleaned each day the court was in session. No "smoke-free" buildings back then! The beautiful old courthouse is still there today.

It is hard to escape the presence of David Crockett in Trenton and Gibson County. A bronze bust of Crockett is on the courthouse lawn, placed there in 1950 by the Tennessee Historical Commission. A replica of his last Tennessee home is in nearby Rutherford, Tennessee, where his mother is buried.

It was Crockett who introduced a bill in the state legislature to create Gibson County. Many of his election speeches were made in Trenton, and it is rumored he made the same remark in

Trenton, as well as Jackson, when he said, "You can go to hell, I am going to Texas!" When Crockett left West Tennessee, he composed a poem. This is one of the verses:

"The home I forsake where my offspring arose;
The graves I forsake where my children repose.
The home I redeemed from the savage and wild;
The home I have loved as a father his child;
The corn that I planted, the fields that I cleared;
The flocks that I raised and the cabin I reared;
The wife of my bosom, farewell to ye all!
In the land of the stranger I ride or I fall."

Crockett left Gibson County, headed for Texas, on November 1, 1835. As he started his journey to the west, Halley's comet passed overhead.

Nathan Bedford Forrest came calling in Trenton on the afternoon of Saturday, December 20, 1862. After capturing the Union garrison in Humboldt the day before, Forrest arrived in Trenton about three o'clock with two hundred and seventy-five men.

Colonel Jacob Fry, the Union commander at Trenton, began preparing earthworks around the depot and concentrated all of the men he could find, including those on sick call. With his position now fortified with bales of cotton, Colonel Fry could hold off any number of attackers. All told, the Federal soldiers had about two hundred and fifty men.

When Forrest arrived, as was his custom he charged straight

ahead, attacking the Federals' position at the Mobile and Ohio Railroad Depot. At first the Confederates were driven back. Changing tactics, Forrest pulled back and began to move troops to the rear and all sides of the depot. When it was completely surrounded, he brought up a battery of artillery and began to shell the depot. The Union forces had no artillery and could not respond. After sixteen rounds were fired, white flags were raised and the battle ended.

When the smoke cleared and the fighting was over, Colonel Fry asked what the terms would be, and Forrest replied, "Unconditional surrender." Colonel Fry, as was the custom, then unbuckled his sword and offered it to Forrest, saying sadly that it had been in his family for forty years. Forrest received the sword and then gave it back, saying, "Take back your sword, Colonel, as it is a family relic; but I hope, sir, when next worn it will be in a better cause than that of attempting the subjugation of your countrymen."

The day had been a complete success from the moment the Confederates arrived in Trenton to the cheers of the townspeople to the Union surrender a short time later. Casualties had been light with only two killed and seven wounded. The list of captured supplies included more than a thousand horses and mules, twenty thousand rounds of artillery, four hundred rounds of small-arms ammunition, a thousand rounds of rations and a huge amount of personal baggage and equipment. Forrest found a very fine sword that he sharpened on both sides and carried throughout the war. Perhaps the most unusual captured item was a supply of counterfeit Confederate money. The troops elected to keep it — it would be wonderful to play poker with!

Before the Union prisoners could be sent north and paroled, Forrest went to a great effort to make them believe his force was much larger than it was. This ruse was accomplished by marching groups of Confederates in from all directions, sending out and receiving phantom communications from fictitious Confederate commanders and burning large numbers of campfires on the outskirts of Trenton.

On Sunday Forrest allowed the citizens to take what they wanted from the Union supplies in the depot before setting it on fire. Nine hundred prisoners were paroled and sent under a flag of truce to the Federal garrison at Columbus, Kentucky. Four hundred Union soldiers from West Tennessee were allowed to go home. After burning the cotton bales and two hundred barrels of pork, Forrest headed north toward Dyer and Rutherford.

It had been a grand two days for the citizens of Trenton. And yet, the war was not over. In many ways, it was just the beginning. Hard times would follow for the next three years. More soldiers would fall on distant battlefields. But for now, it was almost Christmas.

Tennessee Governor William Carroll, a native of Pennsylvania, named Trenton for his beloved Trenton, New Jersey. This Gibson County courthouse dates from 1841 to 1899.

Trenton is the home of the world's largest collection of antique porcelain teapots, given to the city by Dr. Frederick Freed, and insured for eight million dollars. This ceramic couple is representative of the Trenton teapot selection.

Chapter 27

Return to Trenton

If you drive in Trenton, watch your speedometer. But I'm not saying "slow down." I'm saying "speed up." The posted speed limit in Trenton is 31 miles per hour! It's been that way since the 1950s and surely must be the only town in West Tennessee with such a speed limit.

Trenton is a relatively small town in West Tennessee with a population of less than five thousand people. But for a city of that size, it has more than its share of historic events and people. The early history centers on David Crockett and Nathan Bedford Forrest, but there is much more than that. Let's look at some of the people who gave Trenton its history.

Facebook video library
https://goo.gl/nKdgqC

Peter Taylor, author

Peter Matthew Hillsman Taylor was born in Trenton. His father, "Red" Taylor, was a prominent attorney who played football for Vanderbilt. His grandfather Colonel Robert Zachary Taylor fought in the Civil War under General Forrest. Colonel Taylor is best remembered as one of two attorneys who were kidnapped by the Night Riders of Reelfoot Lake and barely escaped being hung. His fellow attorney was killed.

After the Taylor family moved to Memphis, Peter attended Rhodes College (then named Southwestern) and Vanderbilt before transferring to Kenyon College in Gambier, Ohio, to study under the great critic and poet John Crowe Ransom.

He is considered to be one of America's finest short-story writers. He also wrote three novels, including *A Summons to Memphis*, which won the Pulitzer Prize for fiction. His collection *The Old Forest and Other Stories* won the PEN/Faulkner Award. For many college students, even today, Peter Taylor's short stories and novels are required reading.

Wallace Wade, football coach

Wallace Wade was born in Trenton in 1892. One of nine children, he grew up on the family farm. He first played football at Peabody High School in Trenton. Following high school, he attended Brown University in Providence, Rhode Island, where he played guard on the football team.

Following college, he was an assistant football coach and

head basketball coach at Vanderbilt University. After coaching in Nashville, he was hired as head football coach at the University of Alabama. Over the next seven years, Alabama won three national championships. Wade then shocked the coaching world by leaving Alabama and taking the head-coaching job at Duke University, where he coached for sixteen years and his teams won 116 games with only 36 losses.

Wade was inducted into the College Football Hall of Fame in 1955. Duke's football stadium was renamed Wallace Wade Stadium in 1967. A bronze statue of Wade resides outside of Alabama's Bryant-Denny Stadium with statues of three other coaches who have won national championships at Alabama.

Alfred M. Bettis, technology pioneer

Alfred M. Bettis is another Trenton native. He graduated from Peabody High School in 1942. Following high school, he received an appointment to the U.S. Naval Academy. Upon graduation three years later, he was assigned to a squadron of small landing ships carrying ammunition to support an invasion of Japan. It was considered to be a one-way trip because one hit from a Japanese shell would have blown up the ship. The mission ended when Japan surrendered.

Bettis was one of the pioneers of the digital age. A military veteran, his work changed our modern lives forever with computers. He played a major role in the development of shipboard computer systems called NTDS (Naval Technical Data Systems).

Bettis retired from the Navy in 1975 after thirty years and one month of service. Bettis signed up with Sperry-Univac and worked for them in Europe for eleven years. When he finally retired, he returned to his hometown of Trenton and lived on College Street until he died in 2012.

Fred Culp, teacher and historian

Fred Culp was born in the last half hour of December 1927. He often joked about almost missing that year when it was time for his birthday. His father owned a store in nearby Edison. When they told stories about "the old days," Fred would listen and remember the stories. When he got old enough, he looked them up and found one of them was actually true! After graduating from Lambuth College, Fred returned to Trenton to teach history at Peabody High School, where he remained for almost four decades. One of his students said, "He made Tennessee history so interesting. I could have listened to him all day."

For fifty-seven years, Culp was the Gibson County historian. He was the co-author of *Gibson County Past and Present*, the only history of Gibson County. In 2016, he founded the Fred Culp Historical Museum, located inside the Trenton City Hall. Mr. Culp died in July 2017, and much of Gibson County history died with him.

Porcelain teapots

Trenton is the home of the world's largest collection of antique porcelain teapots. The correct name is Veilleuses-theieres, but if you are from Tennessee, you know them as teapots. The collection of 525 teapots was a gift to the city of Trenton from Dr. Frederick Freed, a native of Trenton. Dr. Freed collected the teapots over a 45-year time frame while traveling through Europe, Asia and Northern Africa.

These vessels were used from the mid-1700s through the mid-1800s in sick rooms and nurseries. The earliest veilleuses, or teapots, were made as food warmers with a bowl rather than a teapot. The teapots replaced the bowl and the teapots came into use. They were used to serve floral or herb tea to babies during night hours. They offered the advantage of giving a warm medication to a restless child but also offered a light in the darkness, as the teapots were used long before the invention of electricity. Because of their age and beauty, the teapots are quite valuable. The collection is insured for eight million dollars.

Every year the city of Trenton holds a two-week "teapot festival." The festival begins with the ceremonial Lighting of the Teapots and ends with the Trenton Teapot Festival Annual Grand Parade.

As part of the New Deal, the Civilian Conservation Corps was established in 1933 as a public work relief program for young men, ages eighteen through twenty-five. The Civilian Conservation Corps provided shelter, clothing, food and a monthly wage of thirty dollars, twenty-five dollars of which had to be sent home to their families.

Chapter 28

CCC Camp 499

The Great Depression began in the United States with the fall of stock prices in early September 1929 followed by the market crash on October 29, forever known as Black Tuesday. In response to the economic crisis, Congress and newly elected President Franklin Delano Roosevelt passed a series of programs, including Social Security. The programs, referred to as "The New Deal," focused on what historians refer to as "the three Rs," relief, recovery and reform.

As part of the New Deal, the Civilian Conservation Corps was established in 1933. It was a public work relief program for young men, ages eighteen through twenty-five. It was designed to provide jobs, and at the same time, it implemented a natural resources program in every state and territory. Maximum

Facebook video library
https://goo.gl/nKdgqC

enrollment at any one time was 300,000. Over the course of its nine years of operation, three million men were participants. The Civilian Conservation Corps provided the young men with shelter, clothing, food and a monthly wage of thirty dollars, twenty-five dollars of which had to be sent home to their families.

The program also provided a public awareness of our natural resources and the need to protect them. During its nine years, nearly three billion trees were planted, along with construction projects in state and national parks.

The CCC, as it was known, came to West Tennessee when camps were opened in Jackson, Dyer, Brownsville, Dresden and McKenzie. Two years later, new locations opened in Paris, Selmer, Lexington and Camden. The last to open was in Bolivar in June 1939. Seventy-seven camps were opened in Tennessee.

On April 13, 1933, the Jackson Sun had an article on the front page as arrangements were announced to send recruits to military installations across the country to prepare them for their new assignments. On June 26, two hundred and twenty young men in eight new Chevrolet trucks and two large Army transport vehicles arrived in Jackson. Most of the new recruits were from Mississippi. Accordingly the new camp was named Camp Pat Harrison, honoring a senator from Mississippi. It was designated as Company 499.

The men bivouacked at the current site of North Side High School until a permanent camp could be constructed across the road where Ace Hardware now stands. At the time the five-acre site was covered with bushes and small trees, plus a large amount of trash, all of which had to be hauled away before construction could begin. Clearing the land took almost two months. No heavy equipment was available, and the work had to be done by hand. During this period, the meals were cooked in the fields where the men were working. One recruit remembered eating his food while sitting on stumps or anthills.

John V. Sargent, a native Mississippian and longtime Jackson resident, supervised the construction of the buildings, which consisted of barracks, mess hall, recreation hall, officers' quarters, storage buildings, water tower, garages, infirmary and laundry/shower buildings. During the eight years the camp was operational, several hundred residents of Jackson volunteered to work at the camp.

In today's world, it is hard to imagine working for thirty dollars a month. And yet it is even harder to imagine how people were struggling to survive then. Kenneth Grissom, a prominent Jackson homebuilder, recalled, "I was making fifty cents a day working on the farm." By working at the camp, he doubled his salary. He also remembered his first day at the camp. After receiving his uniforms, he fainted when he was given a smallpox shot during his physical.

Enrolling as a volunteer in the CCC was similar to joining the Army in some ways but less restricted in others. When you joined the CCC, you underwent a physical and suffered through a number of shots. But unlike the Army, there was no "boot camp" training.

C.L. Upton remembered his first day in the winter of 1938 when more than two hundred naked boys crowded into a frigid recreation hall to undergo their physical examinations. Cecil

Flowers remembered being good-naturedly called "son of a bitch" for the first week.

Every enrollee received wool and cotton khaki uniforms, along with tall shoes, long underwear, linens and personal items such as a razor, toothbrush, sewing kit and shoe-shining materials. Enrollees enlisted for a period of six months, and could re-enlist for three more six-month periods. The camps operated under the joint jurisdiction of the soil conservation department and the U.S. Army.

Enrollees spent forty hours a week planting trees or building earthen dams to prevent soil erosion. By 1934 one thousand thirty-nine dams had been completed and ten and a half acres of pines and locusts planted. By 1937 over twelve thousand dams had been completed and the nursery the men built produced forty-five million trees.

Essential to the camp's operation and morale was the food the men received: A traditional full-course breakfast, hot lunch served in the field and supper with hot rolls and cobblers to complete the day. Many of the men gained weight. The menu for a typical day of November 4, 1937, had ham omelet and hot biscuits for breakfast, lamb stew with cornbread and cherry cobbler for lunch, and roast lamb, hot rolls and pineapple pie for the evening meal. Not at all what you would expect.

In 1937 the camp was renamed Camp Herron Pearson for Jackson's popular four-term U.S. congressman. Despite his support, the number of enrollees began to decline. In March 1940, President Roosevelt ordered the transfer of forty-five motor repair shops from the CCC to separate locations. The Jackson

Motor Repair Shop was located at the corner of Garneal and Oneal Street. That building is still standing. By 1941 company strength had been reduced from two hundred and twenty to one hundred and sixty. As the number of men declined, the condition of the camp began to deteriorate.

In April, Jacksonians were shocked to learn the camp was to be relocated to Portland, Tennessee. Despite citizen protests and appeals from Congressman Pearson and Senator Kenneth McKellar, the camp was closed and moved to Portland on October 4, 1941. Of the original seventy-seven CCC camps in Tennessee, only thirty were left.

As war in Europe loomed, many of the enrollees went into the Army. On June 30, 1942, the Civilian Conservation Corps came to an end and all of the camps were closed.

The Civilian Conservation Corps had been a grand experiment. Jackson was better off because of the opportunities that had been presented to the young men who enrolled as well as the conservation programs they created. But now it was time to turn from conservation to fighting World War II.

Several days ago, I drove out to the old CCC campsite on North Highland Avenue. As expected, there is no trace of the camp. The land is now covered in vines and trees, and there is no clue that CCC Camp 499 ever existed. And yet hundreds of young men, over a nine-year period, avoided poverty, helped restore the land and got ready to become soldiers for the war that awaited them.

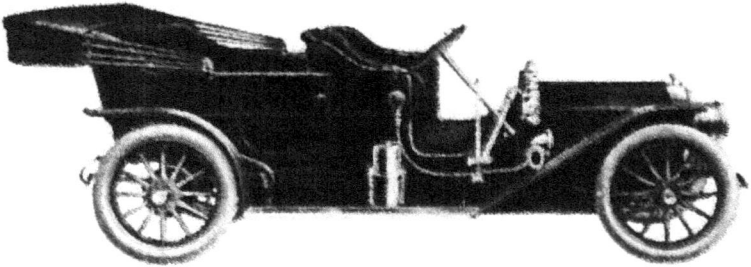

Most people have forgotten that the Marathon automobile was manufactured on North Royal Street at the Southern Engine and Boiler Works between 1906 and 1910. It was the first automobile to be manufactured in the South.

Chapter 29

Shoulda Coulda Woulda

How many times a day do you say, "I should have done that" or "I could have done that," or "I would have done that?" It's the type of game I often play with our history. For example, I often wonder if we still had a vibrant railroad industry as we once did, how would that affect West Tennessee today? What would West Tennessee be like if Interstate 40 had not come through? The list is endless with these types of questions. Let's look back at our history. What would, or could, or should have occurred if these things happened?

Facebook video library
https://goo.gl/nKdgqC

The Flying Machine

In 1858, three years before the Civil War, Isham Walker, an eccentric professor from Spring Creek, tried to get a patent for a flying machine named the "Giant Trout."

It consisted of three giant balloons held together with wire and sheet copper. It was designed to travel three hundred miles an hour more than two miles from the earth's surface.

Congress turned down Walker's request for a million dollars to purchase the materials, and the project died. It would be forty-five years before the Wright Brothers' first flight.

Improbable as it was at the time, what if he had been able to achieve his dream?

Another West Tennessee inventor, F.E. Earnshaw, built an airplane similar to the Wright Brothers. The engine was too heavy for the aircraft, and the experiment failed.

Three years later, the Wright Brothers flew their plane. But what if Walker or Earnshaw had been successful? Could we have been Kitty Hawk?

The State's First Automobile Factory

In 1985 General Motors Company — Saturn — announced it would build a giant industrial plant in Spring Hill, thirty miles south of Nashville. The site covered 2,400 acres.

Most people have forgotten that the Marathon automobile was manufactured on North Royal Street at the Southern Engine and Boiler Works between 1906 and 1910. It was the first automobile to be manufactured in the South.

Not realizing the importance of the automotive industry, its owners sold the company to a group of Nashville investors. Could we have been Spring Hill?

Crockett Lost the Election

In the congressional election of 1836, Adam Huntsman defeated David Crockett by 252 votes. Prior to the election, Crockett had been on a trip to Baltimore, Philadelphia, Boston and New York testing his chances of being elected president of the United States in 1836. As a result, he did not spend as much time campaigning in Tennessee and lost the election to Huntsman. It ruined his chances of being elected president and sent him to The Alamo.

Could he have been elected president of the United States rather than Martin Van Buren? Would The Alamo have been the same without Crockett?

General Grant's reinforcements at The Battle of Shiloh

West Tennessee has no better example of what might have been or perhaps what should have been than the Battle of Shiloh.

When Albert Sidney Johnston decided to attack Union forces at Shiloh, he had just over forty thousand men, roughly the same number of Grant's soldiers encamped at Pittsburg

Landing. However, the Army of the Ohio had another eighteen thousand men on the way to join them. This would give the Union Army a 3-2 advantage.

For the South to win the battle, General Ulysses S. Grant had to be defeated before the Army of the Ohio arrived.

Two months before Shiloh, Confederate forces at Fort Donelson had surrendered to General Grant's army. More than twelve thousand Confederates were marched away to Federal prison camps. Another seven thousand Confederates were captured at the Battle of Island Number Ten on the Mississippi River. If these two groups had not been captured, Johnston would have had another twenty thousand soldiers and a big advantage over Union forces.

Simply put, Grant's army had to be defeated before they were reinforced by the Army of the Ohio. The Confederate Army was only eighteen miles away in Corinth, Mississippi, when they started their march to Shiloh. Because of heavy rain, muddy roads and confusion, it took them longer than expected to reach their position of attack.

If the battle could have started on April 5, rather than April 6, Grant could have been defeated before the Army of the Ohio forces arrived.

But what would have happened, what could have happened if the Confederate Army had been successful? Grant's career would have been ruined. He would not have been Lincoln's choice to lead the Union Army. He would not have served eight years as president.

If Shiloh had been a Union disaster, would it be too much to guess that a negotiated peace might have occurred rather than three more years of bloodshed? What would America be like today if the South had won the war?

Memories of Christmas 1938 and 1944 were precious to all who celebrated.

Chapter 30

Christmas Memories 1938 and 1944

The Great Depression began on October 29, 1929, with the collapse of the U.S. stock market. Nine years later, times were better; it was almost back to the good times of the 1920s. As the economy began to recover, a recession hit that caused the unemployment rate to climb back up to nineteen percent. One in five people were still unemployed. One positive note for American workers was the increase of the minimum wage to forty cents per hour for a 44-hour workweek.

By today's standards, prices in 1938 were very low. The average price of a new home was $3,900. A new car could be purchased for $763, and gas was 10 cents a gallon. A loaf of bread was a dime, and you could buy a pound of hamburger meat for 16 cents.

Facebook video library
https://goo.gl/nKdgqC

While the United States seemed to be on the verge of recovery, events in Europe were beginning to unravel. In March of that year, Germany forcibly annexed Austria. Tension between Germany and Czechoslovakia was escalating toward war. Persecution of Jewish people was increasing, and it was becoming obvious that Germany was moving toward World War II. As all of Europe seemed to be on the brink of conflict, Time Magazine named Adolf Hitler as the "Man of the Year," not so much for what he accomplished, but for his world influence.

On lighter notes, America cheered as heavyweight champion Joe Lewis knocked out Germany's Max Schmeling in the first round. Seabiscuit defeated War Admiral in the "race of the century," a horse race that captivated all of America.

The weather in December 1938 was windy and wet. Temperatures were mild with no ice or snow in the forecast. On December 13, Jackson had its first Christmas parade. At the end of the parade was a jolly old man in a sleigh who looked a lot like Santa Claus! On a more somber note, one week later bank robbers in nearby Toone tried to break into the bank vault but failed, leaving their tools behind.

For those who wanted to travel over the holidays, travel by train was inexpensive. Roundtrip to New Orleans on the Rebel was $13.90; it was $9.40 to Jackson, Mississippi, and $13.50 to Mobile, Alabama. For those who wanted to travel by bus, the new Greyhound Bus station was almost complete. If you traveled to Memphis, rooms at The Peabody were $2.00 per day per person.

In Jackson, the Demolay Fraternity and WTJS radio station

gathered two thousand toys for needy children.

For those who had finished their Christmas shopping and had time for a movie, all the downtown theaters in Jackson were open and advertising. Admission was only ten cents, though I can only wonder what they charged for popcorn! The Lakeview Night Club offered dining and dancing on Tuesday, Thursday and Saturday. And, on the day after Christmas, Bal Masque announced it would have a buffet dinner for its members.

Stores would remain open for last-minute shoppers. For only a nickel you could buy a copy of the Jackson Sun and look at all of the ads! Montgomery Ward's had roller skates for 95 cents and ladies' holiday dresses for $2.98.

Tuchfeld's had ladies' stockings for $1.00, flannel robes for $5.00 and men's ties for 50 cents to $1.00. McGee Ross offered a twenty-six piece set of stainless for $3.50, and Holland's offered ladies' purses for as low as $1.00.

A wide variety of food was available for Christmas cooks. Liberty Grocery had turkey for 26½ cents a pound. Butter was 29 cents, eggs were 30 cents a dozen and oysters were 19 cents a pint. Simpsons had a six-pack of Cokes for a quarter, and cigarettes were 15 cents a pack. And for real dining pleasure, Super Jitney Jungle advertised chitterlings for 25 cents a serving!

Lambuth Memorial United Methodist, St. Luke's Episcopal and North Jackson Baptist churches advertised Christmas Eve services.

If you needed a load of coal, People's Coal Company could be reached by calling phone number 76. Christmas would be good that year, though there was much uncertainty for the years ahead. However, People's Coal Company had the best advice at the bottom of its advertisement:

"May the star of hope that led the wise men on their way –
Make your pathway bright with each Christmas day."

Six years later, Christmas 1944 was very different. On June 6, Allied forces had crossed the English Channel at Normandy. Paris was liberated by late August. By December it began to look like the Germans were finished. On December 16, Nazi forces stormed back in what would be called "the Battle of the Bulge." As Christmas drew near, fighting raged across Europe.

On the other side of the world, U.S. forces began the invasion of the Philippines when they defeated Japanese forces at the Battle of Leyte Gulf. For the first time, B-29 bombers began dropping bombs on Tokyo. For soldiers in Europe or the Philippines, it would be a bleak Christmas.

In West Tennessee, gas had risen to 15 cents a gallon, up a nickel from 1938. Bread was still 10 cents a loaf when available. Across America, the average cost of a new home was $3,150. It was a reasonable price, but there weren't many available.

There would be fewer Christmas parties in 1944. Most people ate at home with fruits and vegetables from their "Victory Gardens." Piggly Wiggly had fully dressed hens for 35 cents a pound. B-grade steaks were 33 cents a pound and B-grade roasts were 25 cents a pound. Several stores mentioned having lard for sale.

Smith Funeral Home had an ad on Christmas Eve, adding it also provided ambulance services. Griffin Funeral Home advertised it had served Jackson for ninety-three years.

Prices for a trip to the movies had doubled in the past six years, going from 10 cents to 20 cents. The price of popcorn remained the same. With the war in Europe and Japan taking center stage, dining and dancing were not as popular but were still available at the Lakeview. Alan Green and his orchestra would be playing there on Christmas night. The Green Lantern on the Nashville Highway was open Tuesday through Saturday, and best of all, Joe's Café advertised it would be open until 10 p.m. on Christmas Eve!

The Cotillion Club was planning its annual Christmas party on the 27th when new members would be presented. In past years it had been a dinner and dance. This year there would be no dance as all of the men were away in the Army. High school sororities and fraternities would hold their dances as usual at the National Guard Armory.

In many ways Christmas would remain the same as always. Stockings would be hung, trees would be decorated, and church bells would ring. But the stores that were open that Christmas season are not the stores of today. Read the names of the businesses that wished you a "Merry Christmas" in the Christmas Eve Jackson Sun: Grand Leader, 333 Tire Company, Nolen's Kiddie Shop, G.H. Robertson, Yellow Cab, Rosenbloom's, Stegall's, First National Bank, Kirby Jones Furniture, Beare Ice and Coal, Tuchfeld's, Moore Studio, Lucille Cleaners, Woolworths, Buster Brown Shoe Store, Holland's and Kisber's. Only Moore Studio is still open!

It would take Rudolph to guide Santa to West Tennessee. The weather was bitter cold with temperatures in the low teens.

Snow was expected for Christmas Day.

Jewel Mainord's Tire Service Christmas Eve ad said it best:

"May your Yule log burn brightly with the warm glow of genuine happiness and may peace and good cheer abide in your heart."

Bibliography

Alexander, Harbert. *Old Trails and Tales of Tennessee.* Favorite Recipes Press, Nashville, Tennessee. 2004.

Alexander, Harbert. *Soldiers, Saints and Sinners.* HillHelen Group Publishing Co., Jackson, Tennessee. 2015.

Alexander, Harbert. *Tales of Madison.* Hillsboro Press, Franklin, Tennessee. 2002.

Bowling, Lewis. *Wallace Wade, Championship Years at Alabama and Duke.* Carolina Academic Press, Durham, North Carolina. 2006.

Buckingham, Nash and Brown, William F. *National Field Trial Champions.* Live Oak Press, Camden, South Carolina. 1994.

Calhoun, Frances Boyd. *Miss Minerva and William Green Hill.* The University of Tennessee Press, Knoxville, Tennessee.

Culp, Frederick M. *Gibson County, Past and Present.* Published through Gibson County Historical Society, Trenton, Tennessee. 1961.

Emerson, Myrtle Rose Leggett. *Ancestors ... and the Seeds Still Grow.* Main Street Publishing, Inc., Jackson, Tennessee. 2011.

Featherston, Alwyn. *Saving the Breakout.* Presidio Press, Novato, California. 1993.

Ford, Jesse Hill. *The Liberation of Lord Byron Jones.* Little Brown and Company, Boston, Massachusetts. 1965.

Forrester, R.C. *Night Riders of Reelfoot Lake.* Lanzer Printing Company, Union City, Tennessee. 2001.

Hitchcock, W. Pat. *Forty Months in Hell.* Page Publishing, Jackson, Tennessee. 1996.

Lyman Jr., William J. *Curlew History.* The Orange Printshop, Chapel Hill, North Carolina. 1948.

McClure, Tony Mack. *Cherokee Proud.* Chunannee Books, Somerville, Tennessee. 1999.

Putnam, Norbert. *Musical Lessons, Vol. 1, a Musical Memoir.* Thimbleton House Media, Nashville, Tennessee.

Stillwell, Leander. *The Story of a Common Soldier of Army Life in the Civil War.* Franklin Hudson Printing Co. 1920.

Sword, Wiley. *Shiloh: Bloody April.* William Morrow & Company, Inc., New York. 1974.

Vanderwood, Paul J. *The Night Riders of Reelfoot Lake.* Memphis State University Press, Memphis, Tennessee. 1969.

Williams, Emma Inman. *Historic Madison.* Jackson-Madison County Homecoming '86 Steering Committee. 1986. Printing by Arcata Graphics, Kingsport, Tennessee.

Yellin, Carol Lynn and Sherman, Janann. *The Perfect 36, Tennessee Delivers Woman Suffrage.* Vote 70 Press, Memphis, Tennessee.

Index

The Ames Plantation began in 1901 when Hobart Ames, a wealthy industrialist from North Easton, Massachusetts, purchased 18,567 acres in Fayette and Hardeman counties. He died in 1945, and his wife Julia, who died in 1950, established a foundation to benefit the University of Tennessee.

About the author

Harbert Alexander graduated from Jackson High School in 1957. He earned a bachelor's degree from the Virginia Military Institute in 1961 and a graduate degree from Rutgers University.

He served as an artillery officer in Schweinfurt, West Germany, retiring from the army as a captain. He is a member of the Military Writers Society of America.

He was associated for 24 years with Jackson National Bank, where he served as president of the bank and vice chairman of the holding company. He was appointed president and CEO of Union Planters Bank of Jackson in 1988.

In 1998, Alexander was promoted to the position of regional president for all of the West Tennessee and Arkansas Union Planters banks. He retired from Union Planters on June 30, 2004. Following this, he joined the Bank of Jackson as chairman and chief executive officer, serving in this position until 2010, and now serves on the board of directors.

He served as chairman on the board of Lambuth University, and was the past chairman of the Jackson Energy Authority board and past chairman of the board of Jackson-Madison County General Hospital. He was named Jackson Exchange Club's "Man of the Year" in 1991.

Alexander, the author of five books, has been the Madison County historian for 23 years, and serves on the Tennessee State Museum board, appointed by Governor Bill Haslam.

He is a member of the Military Writers Society of America and has written for numerous magazines such as the *Tennessee Historical Quarterly* and *Ducks Unlimited.*

He is married to Nora Dancy Noe and has three children and six grandchildren.